PRACTICAL GUIDEBOOK ON DATA DISAGGREGATION FOR THE SUSTAINABLE DEVELOPMENT GOALS

MAY 2021

ASIAN DEVELOPMENT BANK

ADB

© 2021 Asian Development Bank
6 ADB Avenue, Mandaluyong City, 1550 Metro Manila, Philippines
Tel +63 2 8632 4444; Fax +63 2 8636 2444
www.adb.org

Some rights reserved. Published in 2021.

ISBN 978-92-9262-774-4 (print); 978-92-9262-775-1 (electronic); 978-92-9262-776-8 (ebook)
Publication Stock No. TIM210117-2
DOI: http://dx.doi.org/10.22617/TIM210117-2

Notes:
In this publication, "$" refers to United States dollars, unless otherwise stated.
ADB recognizes "Korea" as the Republic of Korea and "Vietnam" as Viet Nam.

Cover design by Rhommell Rico.

CONTENTS

TABLES, FIGURES, AND BOXES

Boxes

FOREWORD

To build a road map for people and the planet and to support sustainable social and economic progress worldwide, the 2030 Agenda for Sustainable Development was launched in 2015 as a universal call to action for ending poverty, protecting the planet, and ensuring that all people enjoy peace and prosperity. Through the Agenda's principle of "leaving no one behind" (LNOB), the member states of the United Nations have committed to eradicating poverty in all its forms, ending discrimination and exclusion, and reducing inequalities and vulnerabilities. Understanding which population groups are left behind and designing effective policies require that the Sustainable Development Goal (SDG) indicators be disaggregated by income class, gender, ethnicity, geographic location, disability status, migration status, and other relevant dimensions. However, disaggregation of the SDG indicators imposes significant data requirements and operational challenges for national statistical systems (NSSs).

In many countries, development data are compiled as national, subnational, or city averages, which paints what would seem to be a society-wide picture with respect to specific development targets. However, these aggregate data do not provide adequate information on which segments of a country's population have made significant progress or have lagged in terms of development. From a policy perspective, the lack of disaggregated data is problematic because there are limited data to guide the design of intervention programs that are meant to appropriately target vulnerable segments of society. On the other hand, where disaggregated data are available, evidence suggests that the most vulnerable groups are likely to benefit less from the development process than the rest of the population, contributing to widening inequalities within countries. Worryingly, during periods of uncertainty such as the ongoing coronavirus disease (COVID-19) pandemic, sparse data suggest that the poor and other vulnerable groups also tend to be at greater risk of social and economic exclusion.

In 2017, the Asian Development Bank (ADB) designed the technical assistance project *Data for Development* to strengthen the capacity of national statistics offices (NSOs) in the Asia and Pacific region to meet the increasing data demands for SDG monitoring and effective policy making. One component of the project focuses on providing guidance on how NSSs can enhance the compilation of disaggregated data for development. As part of this initiative, statisticians from ADB's Statistics and Data Innovation Unit within the Economic Research and Regional Cooperation Department worked with the Statistics Division of the United Nations Department of Economic and Social Affairs (UN DESA) and other development partners to draft this practical guidebook that can be used by staff of NSOs and other organizations that compile SDG indicators and other data for development. In particular, the guidebook provides tools to collect, compile, analyze, and disseminate disaggregated data. Also, it provides background materials regarding issues and experiences of countries regarding data disaggregation for the SDGs. This guidebook is intended for statisticians as well as other analysts from planning and sector ministries involved in the production, analysis, and communication of disaggregated data.

The publication team was led by Arturo Martinez Jr. under the overall direction of Elaine Tan. The preparation of this guidebook began as a series of notes from the International Workshop on Data Disaggregation for the SDGs, organized by the Statistics Division of the UN DESA in Bangkok in January 2019. These notes, which were summarized by ADB consultant Jose Ramon Albert with the assistance of Arturo Martinez Jr., served as one of the main references in finalizing the guidebook. ADB consultant Margarita Guerrero wrote the guidebook, with guidance and inputs provided by Heather Page and Yongyi Min of the United Nations Statistics Division (UNSD); and Arturo Martinez Jr., Mildred Addawe, Marymell Martillan, Joseph Bulan, and Ron Lester Durante of ADB. Several United Nations agencies provided input on tools and resources, including the World Health Organization (WHO), United Nations Entity for Gender Equality and the Empowerment of Women (UN Women), UN Economic and Social Commission for Asia and the Pacific (ESCAP), and United Nations Children's Fund (UNICEF). The Inter-agency and Expert Group on SDG Indicators (IAEG-SDGs) also provided comments on the drafts and has encouraged widespread dissemination of the guidebook, including as a background document to the 52nd session of the UN Statistical Commission (UNSC) in March 2021. Arman Bidarbakht-Nia (ESCAP), Kaushal Joshi (ADB), Sara Duerto Valero (UN Women), Ahmad Reza Hosseinpoor (WHO), and Francois Fonteneau (Partnership in Statistics for Development in the 21st Century [PARIS21]) all contributed to works that were used as inputs and references for this guidebook. Rose Anne Dumayas provided operational support throughout the project. Rhommell Rico designed the cover of this guidebook; Jason Beerman provided editing services, ensuring coherence and consistency; and Jonathan Yamongan carried out layout, page design, and typesetting.

The goal of this practical guidebook is to share knowledge that can improve the capacity to produce, analyze, and communicate disaggregated data for the SDGs. This guidebook is designed to be an initial publication that features analytical tools on producing and using disaggregated data based on the experiences of countries, the IAEG-SDGs, and international and regional organizations. Subsequent updates of this guidebook will be available on the IAEG-SDGs and ADB websites.

The authors' aim is for this document to be a useful reference for delivering high-quality, granular, and cost-effective data for SDG monitoring.

ABBREVIATIONS

ADAPT	Advanced Data Planning Tool
ADePT	Automated Development Economics Poverty Tables
ADB	Asian Development Bank
CBMS	Community-Based Monitoring System
CGD	citizen-generated data
DHS	Demographic Health Surveys
EPIC	Every Policy Is Connected
ESCAP	Economic and Social Commission for Asia and the Pacific
ESCWA	Economic and Social Commission for Western Asia
FAO	Food and Agriculture Organization of the United Nations
FIES	Family Income and Expenditure Survey
HEAT	Health Equity Assessment Toolkit
HIV/AIDS	human immunodeficiency virus/ acquired immunodeficiency syndrome
HRBAD	human rights-based approach to data
IAEG-SDGs	Inter-agency and Expert Group on SDG Indicators
LNOB	leave no one behind
LSMS	Living Standards Measurement Study
MDS	Model Disability Survey
NHTS-PR	National Household Targeting System for Poverty Reduction
NSDS	National Strategies for the Development of Statistics
NSO	national statistics office
NSS	national statistical system
OHCHR	Office of the High Commissioner for Human Rights
PARIS21	Partnership in Statistics for Development in the 21st Century
PSA	Philippine Statistics Authority
SAE	small area estimation
SDG	Sustainable Development Goal
SDMX	Statistical Data and Metadata Exchange
UN	United Nations
UNSC	United Nations Statistical Commission
UNSD	United Nations Statistics Division
UNECE	United Nations Economic Commission for Europe
UNICEF	United Nations Children's Fund
UN Women	United Nations Entity for Gender Equality and the Empowerment of Women
VNR	voluntary national review
WHO	World Health Organization

INTRODUCTION

Background and Rationale

The "leave no one behind" (LNOB) principle is a central crosscutting focus of the 2030 Agenda for Sustainable Development, through which United Nations member states have committed to the following:

> As we embark on this great collective journey, we pledge that **no one will be left behind**. Recognizing that the dignity of the human person is fundamental, we wish to see the Goals and targets met for all nations and peoples and for all segments of society. And we will endeavor to reach the furthest behind first.[1]

Monitoring all targets **requires detailed disaggregation of measures of progress by groups** to ensure that progress toward these targets is reached by all. In addition, some goals (e.g., the goals to eliminate poverty, hunger, and preventable child mortality) are directly concerned with those currently left behind (i.e., the **vulnerable populations**). For instance, the goal on (income) inequality calls for a reduction in disparities, where improvements in the well-being of those left behind will be an important strategy, and the goal on strengthened gender equality focuses on women and girls who are left behind.[2]

Ensuring that these commitments are translated into well-reasoned, evidence-based policies and corresponding effective actions requires a precise understanding, definition, and identification of the target populations. To properly measure progress in attaining the targets and goals, data needs to be collected and statistics need to be generated for clearly defined target populations.

To this end, the United Nations Statistical Commission (UNSC),[3] charged with developing the overall measurement framework and indicators for progress monitoring of the 2030 Agenda, embraced an

---

[1] United Nations (UN). 2015. *Transforming our world: the 2030 Agenda for Sustainable Development* (para. 4). 21252030 Agenda for Sustainable Development web.pdf (un.org).

[2] For an overview of issues on understanding the concept of LNOB and problems involved in its operationalization, refer to S. Klasen and M. Fleurbaey. 2018. Leaving no one behind: Some conceptual and empirical issues. *Committee for Development Policy Background Paper.* 44.
https://www.un.org/development/desa/dpad/wp-content/uploads/sites/45/publication/CDP_BP44_June_2018.pdf.

[3] The UNSC is the highest decision-making body for international statistical activities, responsible for setting statistical standards and developing concepts and methods, including their implementation at the national and international levels. UNSC. https://unstats.un.org/unsd/statcom/.

overarching principle of data disaggregation in the development of the global indicator framework for the Sustainable Development Goals (SDGs) and targeted the following:

> *Sustainable Development Goal indicators should be disaggregated, where relevant, by income, sex, age, race, ethnicity, migratory status, disability and geographic location, or other characteristics, in accordance with the Fundamental Principles of Official Statistics.*[4]

Disaggregation of SDG indicators along these dimensions imposes significant data requirements and operational challenges for national statistical systems (NSSs). Thus, the UNSC created the Inter-agency and Expert Group on Sustainable Development Goal Indicators (IAEG–SDGs) to develop and implement the global indicator framework for the goals and targets of the 2030 Agenda.[5] Implementing the indicator framework includes providing necessary statistical standards and tools to assist NSSs in the production of indicators with the recommended levels of disaggregation. This work in progress, introduced in Chapter 1, has resulted in the identification of dimensions or characteristics by which indicators are to be disaggregated (e.g., sex, age, disability) and corresponding categories (e.g., male or female for the sex dimension). The IAEG-SDGs has also defined a minimum disaggregation set (a set that includes all disaggregation dimensions explicitly referenced in the target or indicator name), prepared an overview of standards for data disaggregation, and identified policy priorities of different vulnerable population groups to provide advice on the future focus of data disaggregation.[6]

This guidebook is designed as a knowledge resource that brings together statistical standards and tools that have been and can be utilized by countries to provide disaggregated data for compiling SDG indicators as defined by the IAEG-SDGs' work on data disaggregation. The guidebook also describes analyses that highlight disparities and inequities in key policy areas made possible by the availability of disaggregated data. The intention is to provide a resource that can be referred to as a starting point for undertaking the statistical work required.

Purpose of the Guidebook

For Whom

This guidebook is primarily intended for statisticians and data analysts of national statistics offices (NSOs) as well as planning and sector ministries involved in the production, analysis, and communication of data and statistics in support of inclusive sustainable development, particularly the monitoring of progress in achieving the SDGs. Researchers, academics, civil society organizations, private sector and information providers, and users in national data ecosystems may also find the guidebook useful and relevant.

---

[4] UN General Assembly. 2017. Resolution adopted by the General Assembly on 10 July 2017: Work of the Statistical Commission pertaining to the 2030 Agenda for Sustainable Development Resolution (71/313). New York. https://undocs.org/A/RES/71/313.

[5] Information on the mandate, membership, and work program of the IAEG-SDG. https://unstats.un.org/sdgs/iaeg-sdgs/.

[6] The compilation of data disaggregation dimensions and categories and the policy priorities are living documents, and will be updated as new information is received. More detailed information are available on IAEG-SDGs. Data Disaggregation for the SDG Indicators. https://unstats.un.org/sdgs/iaeg-sdgs/disaggregation/.

For What

This guidebook is intended to provide information on existing statistical sources, methods, tools, and initiatives that address some of the key issues that need to be considered in the production and analysis of data needed for generating disaggregated statistics and indicators and their reporting and communication in order to:

(i)   better understand the concept of disaggregation as applied to data, statistics, and indicators, and the role of disaggregation in formulating, monitoring, and achieving national development goals, including the SDGs;

(ii)   better understand and respond to the policy–data nexus critical to inclusive and LNOB development as espoused by the 2030 Agenda;

(iii) produce data needed for estimating SDG indicators with the specified disaggregation dimensions for indicators for which methods and tools have been developed and demonstrated;

(iv)   use data produced to generate disaggregated statistics and SDG indicators and to carry out multidimensional data analyses that support policy formulation, analyses, and monitoring of the achievement of SDGs;

(v)   effectively present and communicate disaggregated statistics and SDG indicators and the results of multidimensional analyses to target audiences; and

(vi)   strengthen institutional and NSS capacity for production, analyses, and use of disaggregated SDG indicators in areas where most needed.

How

In this guidebook, the term **"disaggregated data"** refers to data that can be used to generate statistics and indicators for population groups defined by (or disaggregated by or broken down further into) one or more dimensions or characteristics (commonly sex, geographic area, and/or age).[7] The results are referred to as disaggregated statistics or indicators. The entire process is referred to as **data disaggregation.**

In the context of the LNOB principle of the 2030 Agenda, the need for disaggregated data is (i) to be able to identify vulnerable groups or populations that are most likely to be left behind, understanding the factors that keep them in or move them out of that position; and (ii) to report on the indicators for these groups to monitor their progress in achieving the development targets and goals.

The guidebook provides information and guidance on applying sources, methods, and tools for data disaggregation and the analysis, use, dissemination, and reporting of the resulting disaggregated statistics and indicators. The information is gathered from various sources, including methodological briefs, guidance notes, and internationally recommended guidelines (where available); work of the various task teams of the IAEG-SDGs; publications of the United Nations (UN), Asian Development Bank (ADB), and other development partners; illustrative examples from country work gathered from presentations at regional and international workshops featuring disaggregation for SDGs indicators; and tools developed and utilized by international development organizations.

---

[7]   A related term is "granular data," which represents the idea of data about smaller chunks or pieces of a larger population.

The guidebook covers the following main topics:

(i) concepts and definitions relating to the data disaggregation process and their mapping to SDG-related dimensions and priorities, based on the IAEG-SDGs' work on data disaggregation;

(ii) integration of policy demands on inclusive and LNOB development with data and illustrative applications of related tools;

(iii) sources of disaggregated data: descriptions, illustrative uses, and summaries of strengths, potential, and limitations;

(iv) LNOB approaches to data analysis: the policy–data nexus and illustrative applications of multidimensional analysis and related tools;

(v) dissemination and communication of disaggregated statistics and indicators: facilitation of access to and utilization of SDG-related data, and presentation and communication approaches and tools for enhancing understanding and use of disaggregated data in monitoring progress in achieving progress in LNOB in the SDGs; and

(vi) knowledge resources for addressing capacity development needs in producing disaggregated data for generating SDG indicators.

Structure of the Guidebook

The guidebook covers the following topics:

Chapter 1 discusses the concept of LNOB and the SDG indicator requirements, and describes the connection to the statistical concept of data disaggregation. The chapter introduces the disaggregation dimensions and categories and the related statistical standards.

Chapter 2 discusses the importance of clearly defining the relevant and appropriate target populations in terms of the data dimensions explicitly or implicitly stated in development goals and targets. The chapter also presents tools that can facilitate the identification of relevant development policies and matching data needs and policy needs. The chapter illustrates the use of disaggregated data in developing nuanced policy to address different vulnerable groups.

Chapter 3 explains and illustrates the known strengths, potential, and limitations of the following statistical sources of disaggregated data considered in the guidebook: censuses; household sample surveys; administrative registers; data generated in the application of small area estimation models; big data, geospatial data, and related data sources; and data produced by applying methods for integrating data sources.

Chapter 4 explains and illustrates basic methods of generating SDG indicators disaggregated by the specified dimensions, and carrying out equity and disparity analyses and some tools that have been developed to do so. The chapter provides illustrative examples of SDG indicators disaggregated according to recommended dimensions as produced by countries and international organizations.

Chapter 5 illustrates practices in reporting, communicating, and enhancing use of disaggregated statistics and analyses, including reporting on SDG indicators, data visualization, and multilevel analyses.

Chapter 6 identifies key issues on why required disaggregated data are often not available and provides information on knowledge products and ongoing capacity development initiatives that may help NSSs to address these issues.

Source References

A list of knowledge resources that provide more details on the topics covered is provided at the end of each chapter. The illustrations and practices are primarily drawn from various regional and global workshops organized by UN agencies covering topics on data disaggregation for the SDGs held during 2018–2020, including the following:

(i)   International Workshop on Data Disaggregation for SDGs, 28–30 January 2019, Bangkok (co-organized by ADB);[8]

(ii)   Second meeting of the Statistical Coordination Group for the 2030 Agenda in Latin America and the Caribbean: Disaggregated data for regional monitoring of the SDGs, 3–5 September 2019, Quito;[9]

(iii) Economic and Social Commission for Western Asia (ESCWA) Regional Workshop on Data Disaggregation for SDGs Indicators, 19–21 November 2019, Istanbul;[10] and

(iv)   Counted and visible: Global conference on the measurement of gender and intersecting inequalities, 26 February 2020, New York.[11]

Future Updates

The guidebook is designed to be an initial publication in a series of compendiums on tools on producing and using disaggregating data, based on the work of various countries, the IAEG-SDGs, and international and regional organizations. As more updated tools and references become available, the guidebook will be updated too. The updated guidebook will be available on the IAEG-SDGs website (footnote 5) and the ADB website.[12]

---

[8]   UN Statistics Division (UNSD). 2019. *International Workshop on Data Disaggregation for SDGs*. 28–30 January 2019. Bangkok, Thailand. https://unstats.un.org/sdgs/meetings/sdg-inter-workshop-jan-2019/.

[9]   Economic Commission for Latin America and the Caribbean. 2019. *Second meeting of the Statistical Coordination Group for the 2030 Agenda in Latin America and the Caribbean: Disaggregated data for regional monitoring of the SDGs*. 3–5 September 2019. Quito, Ecuador. https://www.cepal.org/en/events/second-meeting-statistical-coordination-group-2030-agenda-latin-america-and-caribbean.

[10] UN Economic and Social Commission for Western Asia. 2019. *Regional Workshop on Data Disaggregation for SDG Indicators*. 19–21 November 2019. Istanbul, Turkey. https://www.unescwa.org/events/regional-workshop-data-disaggregation-sdgs-indicators.

[11] UN Women. 2020. *Counted and Visible. Global conference on the measurement of gender and intersecting inequalities*. 26 February 2020. New York. https://data.unwomen.org/news/counted-and-visible-global-conference-measurement-gender-and-intersecting-inequalities.

[12] ADB. https://www.adb.org.

DATA DISAGGREGATION AND THE SUSTAINABLE DEVELOPMENT GOAL INDICATORS

Overview

The 2030 Agenda for Sustainable Development highlights that no one should be left behind. For this to happen, data to measure progress in meeting the Sustainable Development Goal (SDG) targets must provide a level of granularity or *disaggregation* that makes visible the most vulnerable and marginalized people. Depending on their sex, age, education, income, location, and other intertwining factors, people face different constraints. Disaggregated data allows more effective and efficient policies and interventions. This information can show what works well; what needs more attention; and who is being served by policies, programs, and projects.

The Inter-agency and Expert Group on SDG Indicators (IAEG-SDGs) has compiled existing standards, thoughts, and ideas on data disaggregation for the minimum set of data disaggregation dimensions. The IAEG-SDGs classified the disaggregation dimensions of monitoring the SDG indicators into three categories: (i) the minimum set, (ii) other dimensions in addition to the minimum set, and (iii) additional dimensions that international custodian agencies may introduce in the future.

Producing the levels of disaggregation of SDG monitoring indicators needed to better understand the situation of the most vulnerable and marginalized people is a difficult task. National statistical systems (NSSs) need to prepare a strategy to improve the quality, quantity, and availability of disaggregated data and statistics; the strategy should include financing to support capacity to produce and use these data and statistics.

1.1 What Is Data Disaggregation and Why Is It Important?

In this guidebook, the term data disaggregation is used to mean

> ...the breakdown of observations, usually within a common branch of a hierarchy, to a more detailed level to that at which detailed observations are taken. With standard hierarchical classifications, statistics for related categories can be split (disaggregated) when finer details are required and made possible by the codes given to the primary observations (footnote 7).[13]

---

[13] UN. *Glossary of Classification Terms.* https://unstats.un.org/unsd/classifications/bestpractices/glossary_short.pdf.

In contrast, the term data aggregation is used to mean

> ... *the combination of related categories, usually within a common branch of a hierarchy, to provide information at a broader level...With standard hierarchical classifications, statistics for related categories can be grouped or collated (aggregated) to provide a broader picture...* (footnote 13, p. 1).

The "Big Picture" Does Not Always Portray the Full Picture

Compelling human-interest stories often spur collective action. However, simply telling stories without providing data limits assistance to the few subjects of these stories. Data, particularly official statistics, can be used as leverage to speak on behalf of the ones left behind. These statistics should be able to identify who the vulnerable, disadvantaged, marginalized, or socially excluded are; how many they are; and where they are located. This is the minimum amount of information needed for making policies and designing effective intervention programs for marginalized groups. This information enables societies to hold governments accountable when looking at why segments of the population get left behind in the development process.

However, official statistics have been generally made available in the form of aggregated data. When data are aggregated, they provide a "big picture." The focus on the promise to leave no one behind (LNOB) in the 2030 Agenda has highlighted that the big picture does not always portray the full picture. That is, actual living conditions of vulnerable segments of society such as persons with disabilities, people living with precarious health conditions (e.g., HIV/AIDS), indigenous peoples, undocumented migrants, religious minorities, refugees, the uninsured, the elderly, those internally displaced, or those who are in vulnerable working conditions, among others, are hidden—sometimes inadvertently but at other times deliberately through information suppression. As illustrated in Box 1.1, being absent in the data masks the extent of deprivation and disparities these vulnerable segments face, and further exacerbates their vulnerabilities.

Aggregation loses information in the data, as aggregates often hide the disparities that exist between population groups. In contrast, disaggregation involves breaking down data into smaller information units. When data are sufficiently disaggregated, multidimensionality and intersectionality of inequalities are better brought to the surface and analyzed.[14]

---

[14] Intersectionality is defined as "the complex, cumulative way in which the effects of multiple forms of discrimination (such as racism, sexism, and classism) combine, overlap, or intersect especially in the experiences of marginalized individuals or groups." *Merriam-Webster English Dictionary*. https://www.merriam-webster.com/dictionary/intersectionality.

Box 1.1: Disaggregated Data Provide a More Nuanced Picture of the Development Landscape

To illustrate how aggregated data can hide important details about the development process, consider two countries, A and B, both with 30% of population living in poverty.

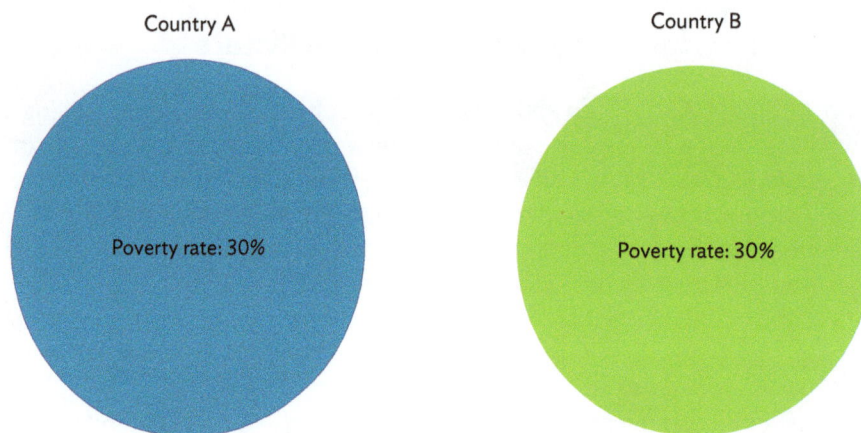

Country A

Poverty rate: 30%

Country B

Poverty rate: 30%

The picture changes if further information is provided: in country B, disparities are more evident when geographic locations are taken into account. The chart shows that the most populous region in Country B also has the highest incidence of poverty.

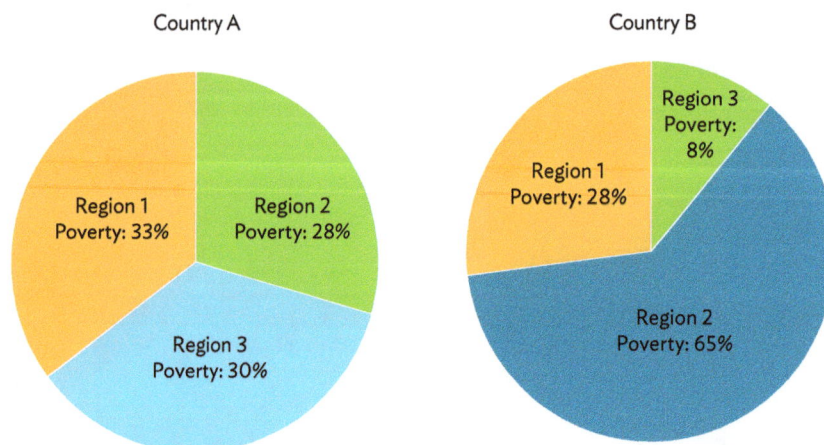

Country A

Region 1
Poverty: 33%

Region 2
Poverty: 28%

Region 3
Poverty: 30%

Country B

Region 3
Poverty: 8%

Region 1
Poverty: 28%

Region 2
Poverty: 65%

Looking further and breaking the data into ethnic groups in each of the regions, it can be seen that inequality is more pronounced within regions in country B.

continued on next page

Box 1.1 *continued*

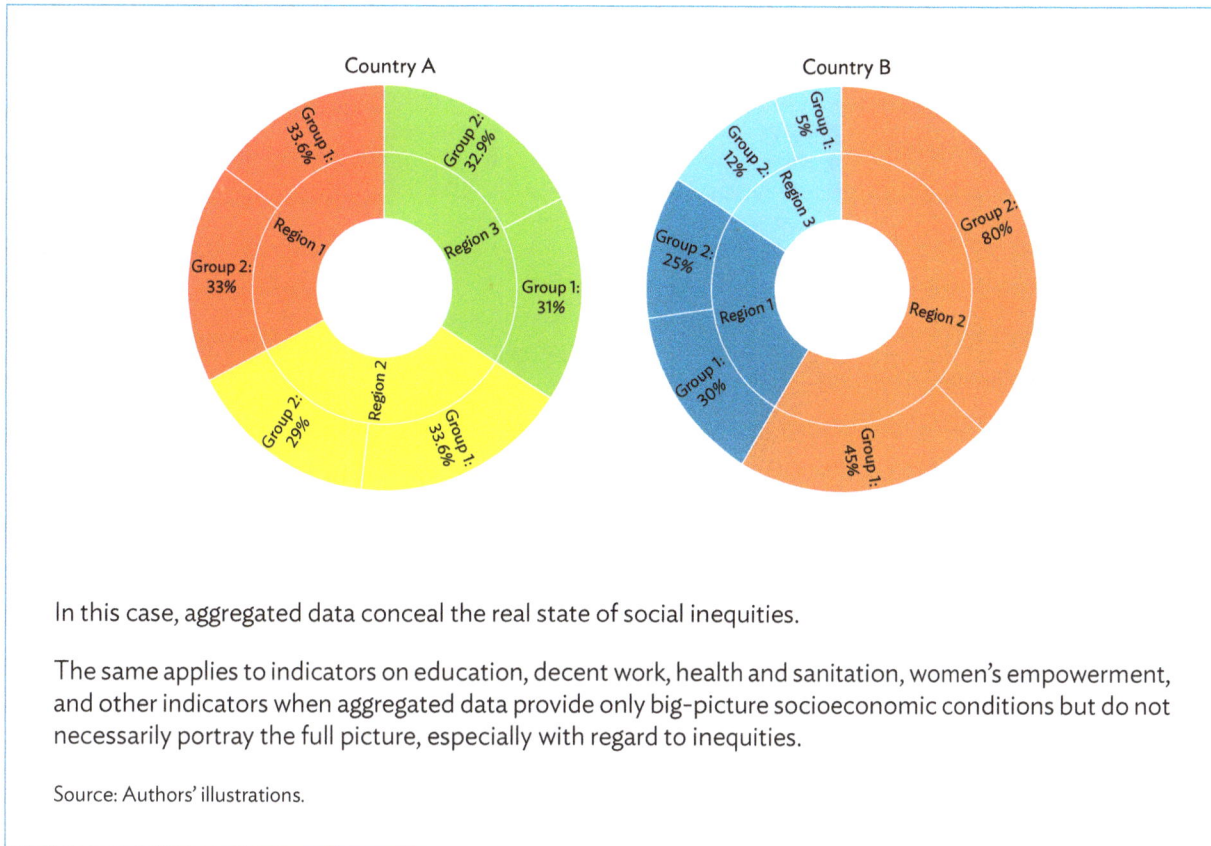

Country A

Country B

In this case, aggregated data conceal the real state of social inequities.

The same applies to indicators on education, decent work, health and sanitation, women's empowerment, and other indicators when aggregated data provide only big-picture socioeconomic conditions but do not necessarily portray the full picture, especially with regard to inequities.

Source: Authors' illustrations.

Discrimination, geography, governance, socioeconomic status, and shocks and fragility are the five key factors that can hide vulnerable groups across societies within aggregated data.[15] These factors can intersect, compounding the deprivations and reinforcing the limitations of people who live in the margins. Consequently, the furthest behind are most likely to endure challenges from multiple and intersecting forms of disadvantages. Even at high levels of disaggregation (e.g., between world subregions, urban–rural, broad age groups), disparities become visible—as shown in Box 1.2.

Policies should be geared to respond to various concerns across demographic groups. People face different constraints depending on their sex, age, education, income, location, and other factors. Information derived from disaggregated data enables more effective and efficient policies and interventions. Data can show what works well, what needs more attention, and who are being served by policies, programs, and projects.

---

[15]   United Nations Development Programme (UNDP). 2018. *What does it mean to leave no one behind? A UNDP discussion paper and framework for implementation.* New York. https://www.undp.org/content/undp/en/home/librarypage/poverty-reduction/what-does-it-mean-to-leave-no-one-behind-.html.

Box 1.2: Even at Coarse Levels of Data Disaggregation, Disparities Can Be Revealed

At the start of the Sustainable Development Goal (SDG) implementation period in 2015, 85% of urban residents globally used safely managed drinking water services, compared to only 51% of their rural counterparts, and 89% of births among the richest quintile were attended by skilled health personnel, compared to 43% among the poorest quintile.

During 2014–2016, the prevalence of undernourishment was significantly higher in least developed countries (27%), landlocked developing countries (23%), and small island developing states (18%) than in the developing regions as a whole (13%). Children from the poorest households are more than twice as likely to be stunted compared to their richest counterparts based on a survey of 87 countries from 2005 to 2014.

In 2015, about three out of five victims of human trafficking in sub-Saharan Africa (65%) and Southeast Asia (57%) are children.

Data from 63 countries surveyed during 2008–2012 showed that children from the poorest households are nearly four times more likely to be out of school than children from the richest households.

Globally, youth aged 15–24 years old are nearly three times more likely to be unemployed than adults 25 years old and over in 2015. Further, youth are also more likely than other age groups to be poor: half of people living in extremely poor households (385 million) were under 18 years.

Across four Asian countries—Bangladesh, Mongolia, Pakistan, and the People's Republic of China—about 90% of women perform unpaid care and domestic work, compared to 31%–75% of men.

Sources:
ADB and UN Women. 2018. *Gender Equality and the Sustainable Development Goals in Asia and the Pacific: Baseline and Pathways for Transformative Change by 2030*. Bangkok. https://www.adb.org/sites/default/files/publication/461211/gender-equality-sdgs-asia-pacific.pdf.
United Nations Statistics Division. 2016. *The Sustainable Development Goals Report*. https://unstats.un.org/sdgs/report/2016/leaving-no-one-behind.
United Nations Statistics Division. 2017. *The Sustainable Development Goals Report*. https://unstats.un.org/sdgs/report/2017/overview/.
World Bank WDI. 2021. https://data.worldbank.org/indicator/SH.H2O.SMDW.RU.ZS (accessed 21 January 2021).

1.2   Disaggregation Dimensions for the Sustainable Development Goal Indicators

The initial work on disaggregation by the IAEG-SDGs identifies disaggregation dimensions and their corresponding categories as follows:[16]

Disaggregation dimensions. *The characteristics by which data are to be disaggregated.*

Disaggregation categories. *The different characteristics under a disaggregation dimension.*

[16]   IAEG-SDGs. 2019. *Data Disaggregation and SDG Indicators: Policy Priorities and Current and Future Disaggregation Plans.* https://unstats.un.org/unsd/statcom/50th-session/documents/BG-Item3a-Data-Disaggregation-E.pdf.

Disaggregation Dimensions

The initial set of disaggregation dimensions defined by the IAEG-SDGs classifies data disaggregation dimensions into three categories:

Category 1. Dimensions mentioned in the goals or targets (also referred to as the minimum set of data disaggregation).

Category 2. Dimensions for which data are currently available (includes other dimensions in addition to the minimum set).

Category 3. Dimensions for which the international custodian agencies may introduce in the future (includes other dimensions in addition to the minimum set).

Table 1.1 presents all of the disaggregation dimensions in the minimum set and the relevant SDG indicators for which data are currently available and will be available in the future.[17]

Table 1.1: Indicators That Disaggregate Data or Have Plans to Disaggregate Data for the Minimum Data Disaggregation Dimensions[18]

Dimension	Current Available	Future Available	Notes
Disaggregation Dimensions Included			
1. Age	1.1.1, 1.3.1, 1.4.1 3.2.1, 3.3.1, 3.3.2, 3.3.4, 3.4.2, 3.5.2, 3.7.1, 3.7.2, 3.a.1 5.2.1, 5.3.1, 5.4.1, 5.5.1 8.5.2 16.2.2	1.2.1, 1.2.2, 1.5.1, 2.1.1, 2.1.2, 2.3.1, 2.3.2 3.1.1, 3.1.2, 3.2.2, 3.3.5, 3.6.1, 3.8.2, 3.9.1, 3.9.2, 3.9.3 4.2.1, 4.3.1, 4.4.1, 4.6.1 5.2.2, 5.3.2, 5.6.1, 5.6.2, 5.b.1 8.5.1, 8.7.1, 8.10.2 9.5.2 10.1.1, 10.2.1, 10.7.1, 11.1.1, 11.2.1, 11.5.1, 11.7.1, 11.7.2 13.1.1, 13.b.1 16.1.1, 16.1.2, 16.1.3, 16.1.4, 16.2.1, 16.2.3, 16.3.2, 16.5.1, 16.6.2, 16.7.1, 16.7.2, 16.9.1, 16.10.1 17.8.1, 17.19.2	1.1.1: Only for employed 1.4.1, 2.3.1, 2.3.2, 3.8.2: Household head 3.1.2: Maternal age
2. Disability Status	1.3.1 8.5.2	1.5.1 5.2.1, 5.2.2 8.5.1 10.2.1 11.1.1, 11.2.1, 11.5.1, 11.7.1, 11.7.2 13.1.1 16.6.2, 16.7.1, 16.7.2 17.19.2	

continued on next page

---

[17] IAEG-SDGs. 2019. *Annex I of Data Disaggregation for the SDG Indicators: Compilation on Data Disaggregation Dimensions and Categories for Global SDG Indicators.* https://unstats.un.org/sdgs/files/Annex%201%20-%20Disaggregation%20Compilation.xlsx.

[18] Updated metadata on the SDGs indicators are in United Nations Statistics Division (UNSD). *E-Handbook on Sustainable Development Goals Indicators.* https://unstats.un.org/wiki/display/SDGeHandbook/Home.

Table 1.1 *continued*

Dimension	Current Available	Future Available	Notes
Disaggregation Dimensions Included			
3. Ethnicity		3.1.1 4.1.1 5.2.1, 5.2.2, 5.3.1, 5.3.2 11.1.1, 11.2.1 16.1.3, 16.3.1	
4. Geographical Location	1.4.1 2.3.1, 2.3.2 4.1.1 5.4.1 6.1.1, 6.2.1 7.1.1 11.6.1, 11.6.2 15.4.2 17.19.2	1.1.1, 1.2.1, 1.5.1, 1.5.2 2.1.1, 2.1.2, 2.4.1 3.2.1, 3.2.2, 3.7.1, 3.7.2, 3.8.1, 3.8.2, 3.b.1 4.2.1, 4.2.2, 4.3.1, 4.4.1, 4.6.1 5.2.1, 5.2.2, 5.3.1, 5.3.2, 5.6.1, 5.b.1 6.4.1, 6.6.1 7.1.2 8.5.2, 8.10.2 9.3.2 10.1.1, 10.2.1 11.1.1, 11.2.1, 11.3.1, 11.5.1, 11.5.2, 11.7.1 13.1.1 16.2.1, 16.2.3, 16.5.2, 16.6.2, 16.7.2, 16.9.1 17.8.1	
5. Income (Wealth)	1.3.1, 1.4.1 3.1.1 10.1.1	1.5.1 3.1.2, 3.2.1, 3.2.2, 3.6.1, 3.8.1, 3.8.2 4.2.1, 4.2.2, 4.3.1, 4.4.1, 4.6.1 5.2.1, 5.2.2, 5.3.1, 5.3.2, 5.6.1 7.1.1 8.10.2 11.1.1, 11.2.1, 11.3.1, 11.5.1, 11.5.2 13.1.1 16.1.3, 16.2.1, 16.2.3, 16.5.1, 16.9.1 17.10.1, 17.11.1, 17.19.2	
6. Migrant Status	4.1.1, 4.6.1 8.8.1	8.8.2 10.7.1 11.1.1, 11.2.1 16.3.1	4.1.1, 4.6.1, 8.8.1, 8.8.2: Migrant or non-migrant 10.7.1: Type of migration process (documented or undocumented)
7. Race		11.1.1, 11.2.1	
8. Sex	1.1.1, 1.4.1 3.2.1, 3.3.1, 3.3.2, 3.4.1, 3.4.2, 3.5.2, 3.a.1 4.1.1, 4.2.2, 4.3.1, 4.4.1, 4.c.1 5.4.1, 5.6.2, 5.b.1 8.3.1, 8.5.1, 8.5.2, 8.6.1, 8.7.1, 8.8.1 16.2.2, 16.2.3, 16.10.1	1.2.1, 1.2.2, 1.3.11.4.2, 1.5.1, 1.b.1 2.1.1, 2.1.2, 2.3.1, 2.3.2 3.2.2, 3.3.4, 3.6.1, 3.8.2, 3.9.1, 3.9.2, 3.9.3 4.2.1, 4.6.1 5.a.1 7.1.1 8.8.2, 8.10.2 9.2.2, 9.3.2, 9.5.2 10.1.1, 10.2.1, 10.7.1 11.2.1, 11.5.1, 11.7.1, 11.7.2 13.1.1, 13.b.1 16.1.1, 16.1.2, 16.1.3, 16.1.4, 16.2.1, 16.3.1, 16.3.2, 16.5.1, 16.5.2, 16.6.2, 16.7.1, 16.7.2, 16.9.1 17.8.1, 17.19.2	1.1.1: Only for employed 1.4.1, 2.3.1, 2.3.2, 3.8.2: Household head 9.3.2, 16.5.2: Manager, ownership

Source: Updated metadata on the Sustainable Development Goal indicators are in United Nations Statistics Division (UNSD). *E-Handbook on Sustainable Development Goals Indicators.* https://unstats.un.org/wiki/display/SDGeHandbook/Home.

Detailed updated information on this as well as the full set of dimensions can be found on the IAEG-SDGs website.[19] The information includes more than 200 other dimensions, presented by goal. These include, for example, education level, employment status, socioeconomic status, and occupation.

Disaggregation Categories

Recommendations on categories for the various dimensions are still works in progress. However, the existing compilations show that a given dimension requires different categories depending on the goal or target and the associated indicator. Two examples are discussed in Table 1.2.

Table 1.2: Illustration of Disaggregation Categories

Indicator	Minimum Required Disaggregation Dimensions	Minimum Required Disaggregation Dimension Available in Global SDG Database (Yes/No)	Disaggregation Category of Minimum Required Disaggregation Dimension
1.3.1 Proportion of population covered by social protection floors/systems, by sex, distinguishing children, unemployed persons, older persons, persons with disabilities, pregnant women, newborns, work injury victims, and the poor and the vulnerable	1. Sex 2. Age 3. Employment status 4. Disability 5. Pregnancy 6. Work injury victims 7. Income	1. No 2. Yes 3. Yes 4. Yes 5. Yes 6. Yes 7. Yes	1. Male or female 2. Children or above retirement age 3. Employed/unemployed 4. People with severe disabilities 5. Mothers with newborns 6. Work injury victims 7. Lowest income quintile
1.4.1 Proportion of population living in households with access to basic services	1. Sex of household head 2. Age of household head 3. Employment status of household head 4. Geographic location (urban or rural) 5. Household incomes	1. Yes (household head) 2. Yes (household head) 3. Yes (household head) 4. Yes 5. Yes	1. Male or female 2. Disaggregated by 5-year age groups from 15+ 3. Employed or unemployed 4. Urban, rural, or city 5. Lowest income quintile

Source: IAEG-SDGs. 2019. *Data Disaggregation for the SDG Indicators*. https://unstats.un.org/sdgs/iaeg-sdgs/disaggregation/; IAEG-SDGs. 2019. *Annex I of Data Disaggregation for the SDG Indicators: Compilation on Data Disaggregation Dimensions and Categories for Global SDG Indicators.* https://unstats.un.org/sdgs/files/Annex%201%20-%20Disaggregation%20Compilation.xlsx.

For indicators 1.3.1 and 1.4.1, the common minimum required disaggregation dimensions are sex, age, and employment status. However, indicator 1.4.1 refers to the sex, age, and employment status of the household head. While sex (male or female) and employment status (employed or unemployed) have the same categories for both indicators, the categories of the variable age differ; that is, the subgroups in the population (the dimensions) identified in indicator 1.3.1 include children and older persons but for indicator 1.4.1, the age categories start with 15+ years (and older) and do not include children.

---

19   IAEG-SDGs. 2019. *Data Disaggregation for the SDG Indicators*. https://unstats.un.org/sdgs/iaeg-sdgs/disaggregation/; IAEG-SDGs. 2019. *Annex I of Data Disaggregation for the SDG Indicators: Compilation on Data Disaggregation Dimensions and Categories for Global SDG Indicators*. https://unstats.un.org/sdgs/files/Annex%201%20-%20Disaggregation%20Compilation.xlsx; and IAEG-SDGs. *Annex II of Data Disaggregation for the SDG Indicators: Summary of Disaggregation Dimensions and Categories Available and Planned in Global SDG Indicator Database*. https://unstats.un.org/sdgs/files/Annex%202%20-%20Disaggregation%20Availability.xlsx.

Overview of Existing Standards

The IAEG-SDGs has compiled existing standards, thoughts, and ideas on data disaggregation for the minimum set of data disaggregation dimensions. The compilation, which is accessible as a living document, provides information for each dimension on the following:[20]

(i)   different categories already in use;
(ii)   information and evaluation of the categories;
(iii)   corresponding categories used in the global indicator framework;
(iv)   existing global standards; and
(v)   existing regional standards.

Information drawn from this compilation for the dimensions of age and ethnicity are shown in Table 1.3.

Table 1.3: Standards for Categories of Age and Ethnicity

Dimensions	Different Categories Already in Use	Information/Evaluation	Categories Used in the Global Indicator Framework	Existing Global Standards
Age	(i) Date of birth (ii) Age groups (iii) 1-year-age-groups	(i) Use of different age groups in national and international data (ii) Differing age groups demanded in indicator or target	Differing age groups: Commonly used categories (i) 15–49 (ii) <15 (iii) 15–49 (iv) >15 (v) 15–65 (vi) <5	United Nations (UN) definition of age groups: (i) Infants: 0–5 years (ii) Children: 0–15 years (iii) Youth: 5–24 years (iv) Adults: 15 years and older (v) Older persons: 60 years and older
Ethnicity	(i) Ethnic ancestry or origin (ii) Ethnic identity (iii) Cultural origins (iv) Race (v) Minority status (vi) Tribe (vii) Language	• UN concepts and definitions: "By the nature of this topic, these categories and their definitions will vary widely from country to country; therefore, no internationally accepted criteria are possible."[21]	Data are not disaggregated by ethnicity	No international standard possible because of varying national circumstances

continued on next page

---

[20]   UNSD. 2018. *Overview of standards for data disaggregation.* https://unstats.un.org/sdgs/files/Overview%20of%20Standards%20for%20Data%20Disaggregation.pdf.

[21]   UNSD. 2001. *Principles and Recommendations for a Vital Statistics System, Revision 2.* New York. p. 37. https://unstats.un.org/unsd/publication/SeriesM/SeriesM_19rev2E.pdf.

Table 1.1 *continued*

Dimensions	Different Categories Already in Use	Information/Evaluation	Categories Used in the Global Indicator Framework	Existing Global Standards
	(viii) Religion (ix) Ethnic self-identification (x) Recognized (national) minorities	• UN standards and methods: "Ethnicity is multidimensional and is more a process than a static concept, and so ethnic classification should be treated with movable boundaries."[22] Caution: different connotation of origin and tribe Disaggregation categories could offend certain population groups.		

Source: UNSD. 2018. *Overview of standards for data disaggregation.* https://unstats.un.org/sdgs/files/Overview%20of%20Standards%20for%20 Data%20Disaggregation.pdf.

1.3   Developing a Strategy for Getting Disaggregated Data

It is difficult to produce the levels of disaggregation of SDG monitoring indicators needed to better understand the situation of the most vulnerable and marginalized people. NSSs need to prepare a strategy to improve the quality, quantity, and availability of disaggregated data and statistics; that strategy should include financing to support capacity to produce and use these data and statistics.

The Inclusive Data Charter is an initiative of the Global Partnership for Sustainable Development Data to mobilize political commitments and meaningful actions to help countries advance disaggregated data.[23] The strategy and preparation of action plans are guided by the five principles described in Figure 1.1.

In general, action plans are monitored on a voluntary basis.[24]

---

[22]   L. Farkas. 2017. *Analysis and comparative review of equality data collection practices in the European Union: Data Collection in the Field of Ethnicity.* Luxembourg, p. 21. https://ec.europa.eu/newsroom/just/document.cfm?action=display&doc_id=45791.

[23]   Global Partnership for Sustainable Development Data. *Inclusive Data Charter vision and principles.* https://www.data4sdgs.org/sites/default/files/2018-08/IDC_onepager_Final.pdf.

[24]   An example of an action plan (for the Philippine Statistics Authority) is here: Global Partnership for Sustainable Development Data. *The Philippine Action Plan on the Inclusive Data Charter.* https://www.data4sdgs.org/sites/default/files/2018-07/PSA%20 IDC%20Action%20Plan.pdf. An example of an annual monitoring report (for the Philippine Statistics Authority) is here: Global Partnership for Sustainable Development Data. *Inclusive Data Charter Initiative (Annual Monitoring) 2019: Philippine Statistics Authority.* https://www.data4sdgs.org/sites/default/files/2019-07/PSA%20-%20IDC%20annual%20monitoring%20form%20 2019.pdf.

Statistics Sweden prepared its first report on the situation of those who are furthest left behind in Swedish society through its annual statistical review process that focused on the LNOB principle.[25] This initial review identified sources, breakdowns, and specific indicators that will be incorporated in future regular statistical reviews, and it adopted the following pragmatic approach: use what we have, use what we know, and learn and develop.

Figure 1.1: Inclusive Data Charter Vision and Principles

Principle One — All populations must be included in the data
We can only achieve the "leave no one behind" goal by empowering the furthest behind. This means ensuring their voices are heard and their experiences are represented through data and analytics. We need to acknowledge all people, make them visible in the data to understand their lives, and include them in the development process.

Principle Two — All data should, wherever possible, be disaggregated in order to accurately describe all populations
We recognize that data should be disaggregated by sex, age, geographic location, and disability status and, where possible, by income, race, ethnicity, migratory status, and other characteristics relevant in national contexts.

Principle Three — Data should be drawn from all available sources
We recognize the need to make high-quality, timely data from official and non-official sources accessible, and that these should include new data sources, where consistent with internationally accepted statistical standards.

Principle Four — Those responsible for the collection of data and production of statistics must be accountable
We will balance the principles of transparency - maximizing the availability of disaggregated data - confidentiality, and privacy to ensure personal data is not abused, misused, or putting anyone at risk of identification or discrimination, in accordance with national laws and the Fundamental Principles of Official Statistics.

Principle Five — Human and technical capacity to collect, analyze, and use disaggregated data must be improved, including through adequate and sustainable financing
We recognize that collecting and analyzing disaggregated data needs specific skills and these must be built. We recognize the need to finance data collection, analysis, and use appropriately and sustainably so that high-quality data can be collected and used by governments as well as by businesses, civil society, and citizens.

Source: Adapted from Global Partnership for Sustainable Development Data. *Inclusive Data Charter vision and principles.* Available from https://www.data4sdgs.org/sites/default/files/2018-08/IDC_onepager_Final.pdf.

---

[25] Statistics Sweden. 2020. *Annual statistical review with a focus on LNOB.* Presentation prepared for the 11th IAEG-SDGs Meeting. 4 November 2020. https://unstats.un.org/sdgs/files/meetings/iaeg-sdgs-meeting-11/13b.%20Sweden-first%20country%20 report%20with%20a%20focus%20on%20vulnerable%20populations_Sweden.pdf.

INTEGRATING POLICY DEMANDS ON INCLUSIVE DEVELOPMENT WITH DATA

Overview

The leave no one behind (LNOB) principle requires that all vulnerable groups are identified and targeted by policies. Striking a balance between policy formulation and demand for data calls for the active involvement of data producers in policy processes. A human rights-based approach to data (HRBAD) allows the collection and publication of disaggregated data. It is toward this end that the Inter-agency and Expert Group on SDG Indicators (IAEG-SDGs) mapped the policy priority targets and indicators to provide countries with concrete suggestions of areas for data disaggregation. This chapter provides an overview of three examples of tools that can facilitate the linking of policies and data: Every Policy Is Connected (EPIC), Advanced Data Planning Tool (ADAPT), and StaTact.

2.1　The Policy–Data Nexus for Leaving No One Behind

With the 2030 Agenda for Sustainable Development, data-driven policy formulation has taken on greater significance. To LNOB, statistical processes must first ensure that everyone is counted. The LNOB principle requires that all target groups likely to be left behind (i.e., the vulnerable groups) be identified and acknowledged by relevant policies and included in the data production and reporting process. Vulnerability is multidimensional, and policy and data need to apply various lenses (social, economic, and environmental) in an integrated manner to correctly zero in on the target vulnerable groups. The hypothetical case described in Box 2.1 illustrates the consequences of not doing so.

Approaches to policy frameworks that integrate the principle of LNOB have included using the principle to guide targeted interventions, or to guide an overall development strategy. Regardless of what is adopted, trade-offs are expected in policy formulation.

A preferential focus on ensuring that no one is left behind can be very costly, as well as politically challenging, and may come at the cost of promoting the efficient use of scarce resources. These trade-offs could result in potential tensions, evident in the following questions. Should infrastructure be focused on underdeveloped areas, even if this means that economic development of the entire country slows down as a result? Should individuals focus on improving the lives of those left behind where they currently live, which may be costly, or increase their opportunities to move to more economically dynamic regions? Should a focus on improving the lives of those left behind take precedence over other goals, such as environmental sustainability? Clearly, these are difficult issues that require detailed country-specific analysis and policy responses that are often difficult, as described in Box 2.2.

Box 2.1: Aura's Case

"Aura is an 85-year-old woman living in South Intopia, the most polluted part of a nameless fictional country, where the economy is dominated by the mining industry. She suffers from acute asthma and earns an equivalent of $2 per day from her husband's pension plan. In recent years, Aura has struggled with her medical expenses and finally decided to sign up for a program that distributes cash to poor families. The country's Ministry of Housing and Poverty identified Aura as ineligible for the program as she earns above the minimum daily income of $1.90. She explained her exceptional condition to the officer from the ministry and was told that she is economically not poor, so her problem had to be taken to the Ministry of Health, where she was told last year that her disease was not on the list of the subsidized medical coverage plan. She was also advised by her doctor to move out of the polluted area. Aura sought support from the Ministry of Social Welfare to relocate her house, but her justification was deemed environmental, which falls outside the mandate of this ministry. Aura was advised to take her issue back to the Ministry of Housing and Poverty, which had already informed her that she was not defined as poor, trapping her in the same futile cycle.

Aura cannot find any place in the government's policy priorities. She is not "left behind" according to data, and is not prioritized by any of the policy programs. Why do the data not show her as a vulnerable member of society? Why has no policy identified her as target and/or vulnerable citizen? And, who should fix the problem: the data producer or the policy maker?

One increasingly necessary conclusion is this: data should be made available in a format that allows the identification, as well as examination, of multiple and intersectional characteristics that define many of those who are left behind."

Source: A. Bidarbakht-Nia. 2018. *Why, What and How of Policy – Data Integration*. Presentation prepared for the Pacific Workshop on Developing a Generic Tool for Policy–Data Integration. Fiji. 19–21 March 2018. https://www.unescap.org/sites/default/files/S3%20 -%20Policy%20Statistics_Data%20integration.pdf.

Box 2.2: Lack of Demand or Lack of Supply?

"Policy-data integration is often a case of the chicken or the egg dilemma."

The lack of demand is considered a main challenge for producing relevant data while insufficient data are accounted for the absence of appropriate policies due to lack of evidence.

The root cause analysis depends on the perspective of the analyst as a data producer or a policymaker.

Since the data producers do not actively engage in discussion on policies and the policymakers do not specify their data needs for monitoring, this has created a vicious cycle where mutual concession between them recurs with little success.

Source: A. Bidarbakht-Nia. 2018. Connecting policymakers and data producers. *United Nations Economic and Social Commission for Asia and the Pacific blog*. 22 August. https://www.unescap.org/blog/connecting-policymakers-and-data-producers.

Policy processes involve different stages, including agenda setting, formulation and implementation, and monitoring and evaluation. Once an issue requiring a policy solution has been identified, the process of policy development includes how an issue is framed by various stakeholders, which issues get prioritized in the policy agenda for a given period, and how the policy is formulated. Decisions at these various stages of policy development, including adjustments to policies, should be better informed by available data and statistics. Policies should also include rational analysis of what works and what does not.

Policies that are based on systematic evidence are widely viewed to produce better outcomes than those not informed by data and statistics. The policy–data nexus, illustrated in Figure 2.1, argues that the absence of appropriate policies can be attributed to data gaps, but lack of demand for data is also a primary challenge for producing relevant data. Whether lack of data is because of lack of demand or lack of supply, it is important for data producers to be part of policy discussions to share their perspectives.

Figure 2.1: The Policy-Data and Data-Policy Nexus

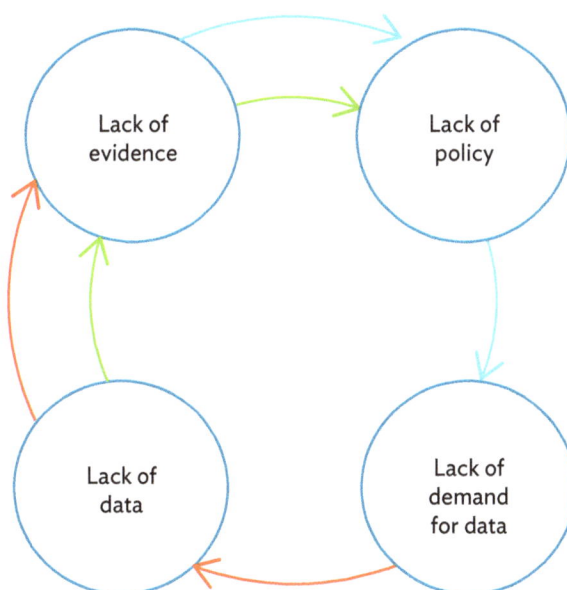

Source: Adapted from A. Bidarbakht-Nia. 2018. Connecting policymakers and data producers. *United Nations Economic and Social Commission for Asia and the Pacific blog*. 22 August. Available from https://www.unescap.org/blog/connecting-policymakers-and-data-producers.

2.2   Disaggregated Data: The Human Rights-Based Lens

The 2030 Agenda for Sustainable Development is unequivocally anchored in human rights with the 17 Sustainable Development Goals (SDGs), 169 targets, and 231 indicators meant to "realize the human rights of all." It is explicitly "grounded in the United Nations Charter, the Universal Declaration of Human Rights, international human rights treaties" and other instruments, including the Declaration on the Right to Development (footnote 1, p. 3).

Data collection and disaggregation that allow for comparison of population groups or characteristics are central to an HRBAD and forms part of states' human rights obligations, i.e., to collect and publish data disaggregated by grounds of discrimination recognized in international human rights law.[26]

The HRBAD guidance note states the following:

> *As devising disaggregation of indicators (or not) is not a norm or value neutral exercise, and the risks associated with this operation for the protection of the rights of data subjects cannot be denied, an HRBAD has much to offer in this context. As outlined in this note, an HRBAD helps bring together relevant data stakeholders and develop communities of practice that improve the quality, relevance and use of data and statistics consistently with international human rights norms and principles* (footnote 26, p. 2).

Components of a Human Rights-Based Approach to Data

An HRBAD identifies a preliminary set of principles, recommendations, and good practices under each of the following six interrelated components (Figure 2.2):

(i)   **Participation.** Relevant population groups should participate in data collection exercises, including planning, data collection, dissemination, and analysis of data.

(ii)   **Data disaggregation.** This allows data users to compare population groups, and to understand the situations of specific groups.

(iii) **Self-identification.** For the purposes of data collection, populations of interest should be self-defining. Individuals should have the option to disclose, or withhold, information about their personal characteristics.

(iv)   **Transparency.** Data collectors should provide clear, openly accessible information about their operations, including research design and data collection methodology. Data collected by State agencies should be openly accessible to the public.

(v)   **Privacy.** Data disclosed to data collectors should be protected and kept private, and confidentiality of individuals' responses and personal information should be maintained.

(vi)   **Accountability.** Data collectors are accountable for upholding human rights in their operations, and data should be used to hold states and other actors to account on human rights issues.

---

[26]   United Nations (UN) Office of the High Commissioner for Human Rights (OHCHR). 2018. *A Human Rights-Based Approach to Data: Leaving No One Behind in the 2030 Agenda for Sustainable Development—Guidance Note to Data Collection and Disaggregation.* Geneva. https://www.ohchr.org/Documents/Issues/HRIndicators/GuidanceNoteonApproachtoData.pdf.

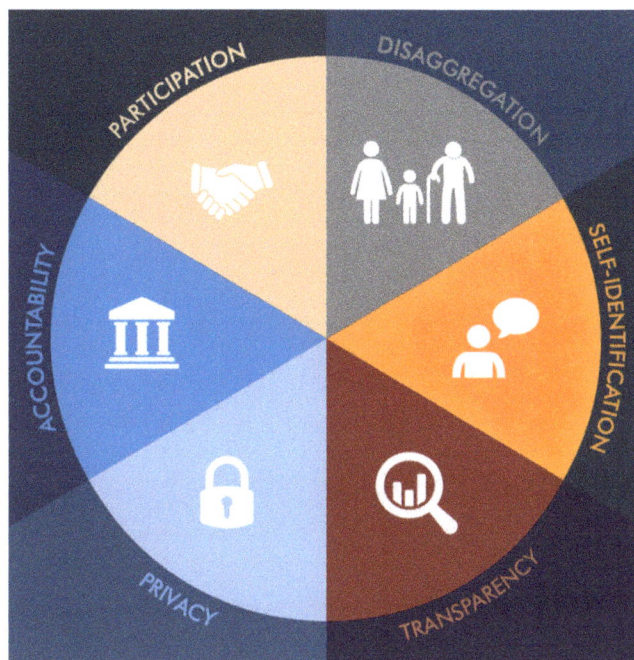

Figure 2.2: Six Components of a Human Rights-Based Approach to Data

Source: Adapted from United Nations Office of the High Commissioner for Human Rights. 2018. *A Human Rights-Based Approach to Data: Leaving No One Behind in the 2030 Agenda for Sustainable Development*. Geneva. Available from https://www.ohchr.org/Documents/Issues/HRIndicators/GuidanceNoteonApproachtoData.pdf.

Data Disaggregation and the Human Rights-Based Approach to Data Principles

The HRBAD guidance note states the following: *"Data collection and disaggregation that allow for comparison of population groups are central to an HRBAD and forms part of States' human rights obligations. Disaggregated data can inform on the extent of possible inequality and discrimination"* (footnote 26, p. 7).

Per the guidance note, key HRBAD principles on the disaggregation of data are as follows:

More detailed data than national averages is key in identifying and understanding inequalities.

Data should be disaggregated by key characteristics identified in international human rights law.

Collection of data to allow disaggregation may require alternate sampling and data collection approaches.

Birth registration is foundational for robust data sets that allow accurate disaggregation (footnote 26, p.7).

A compilation by United Nations (UN) Office of the High Commissioner for Human Rights (OHCHR) lists human rights standards and recommendations for the following population groups or characteristics:[27]

(i) Gender or sex;
(ii) Age (children, adolescents, older persons);
(iii) Race, color, ethnicity, or national origin or birth;
(iv) Indigenous peoples;
(v) Minorities;
(vi) People of African descent;
(vii) Persons with albinism;
(viii) Migrants, internally displaced persons, or trafficking in persons;
(ix) Geographic status;
(x) Health status and/or HIV/AIDS;
(xi) Disability;
(xii) Religion, belief, and ideology or political affiliation, and/or professional status;
(xiii) Civil status;
(xiv) Income or socioeconomic status; and
(xv) Sexual orientation, gender identity, intersex status, or sex characteristics.

2.3 Vulnerable Groups in the Sustainable Development Goals and Policy Priorities

The global indicator framework for the SDGs and targets as originally developed by the IAEG-SDGs and adopted by the UN General Assembly and its current version reflecting annual refinements identify the populations to be monitored by listing key disaggregation variables in the chapeau, as follows:[28]

Sustainable Development Goal indicators should be disaggregated, where relevant, by income, sex, age, race, ethnicity, migratory status, disability and geographic location, or other characteristics, in accordance with the Fundamental Principles of Official Statistics.

SDG target 17.18 recognizes the need for more systematic data disaggregation, calling on all parties to *"increase significantly the availability of high-quality, timely and reliable data disaggregated by income, gender, age, race, ethnicity, migratory status, disability, geographic location and other characteristics relevant in national contexts"* (footnote 28, p. 21).

Toward this end, the IAEG-SDGs' initial work on data disaggregation included an extensive consultative exercise that identified policy priorities for vulnerable population groups to be defined by application of the dimensions and categories for disaggregation discussed in Chapter 1.2. The consultation aimed to provide a better understanding of what the corresponding policy areas are and to provide advice on the dimensions and categories necessary for disaggregation of these priority areas. The policy priority areas, when mapped to SDG targets and indicators, provide countries with concrete suggestions of areas for data disaggregation. The initial results of this work in progress are briefly summarized in Table 2.1 (footnote 3).

---

[27] UN OHCHR. 2018. *International human rights standards and recommendations relevant to the disaggregation of SDG indicators.* https://unstats.un.org/sdgs/files/meetings/iaeg-sdgs-meeting-07/Human%20Rights%20Standards%20for%20Data%20 Disaggregation%20-%20OHCHR%20-%20Background%20Document.pdf (accessed 9 March 2021).

[28] UN. 2017. *Global indicator framework for the Sustainable Development Goals and targets of the 2030 Agenda for Sustainable Development.* https://unstats.un.org/sdgs/indicators/Global%20Indicator%20Framework%20after%202020%20review_Eng.pdf.

Table 2.1: Policy Priorities for Vulnerable Populations

Population Group	Policy Priorities
Poor	• Inclusive and pro-poor growth • Social protection systems and floors • Effective governance, including participation and use of available resources
Women and girls	• Poverty eradication • Food insecurity and health • Education • Access to economic resources and decent work for all • Gendered impacts of climate change
Children	• Every child survives and thrives • Every child learns • Every child is protected from violence and exploitation • Every child lives in a safe and clean environment • Every child has an equitable chance in life
Older persons	• Health • Income security • Violence, abuse and safety • Empowerment and participation as full members of society
International migrants	• Provide access to basic services (education and health care) and social protection for migrants • Ensure fair recruitment, decent work, and labor rights protection for migrants • Eliminate all forms of discrimination and reduce violence against migrants • Ensure access to information for migrants
Forcibly displaced persons (refugees and internally displaced persons)	• Basic needs and living conditions • Livelihoods and economic self-reliance • Civil, political, and legal rights
Persons with disabilities	• Poverty eradication • Education • Employment • Health • Accessibility

Source: IAEG-SDGs. 2019. *Data Disaggregation and SDG Indicators: Policy Priorities and Current and Future Disaggregation Plans.* https://unstats.un.org/unsd/statcom/50th-session/documents/BG-Item3a-Data-Disaggregation-E.pdf.

2.4   Tools for Policy–Data Integration

This section provides overviews of three sample tools that can facilitate the linking of policies and data: EPIC, ADAPT, and StaTact.

Every Policy Is Connected (EPIC)

Data disaggregation requirements for the SDGs must ultimately be identified in a process of policy–data integration. For this purpose, the development community has developed various policy–data integration tools to assist governments. The UN Economic and Social Commission for Asia and the Pacific (ESCAP) has developed EPIC, a tool for reviewing the data needs for monitoring national policies. The tool is based on a framework for a structured, participatory, and principle-based dialogue between policy and data stakeholders.[29]

The framework first defines a policy–data landscape and identifies (i) gaps (lack of demand, supply, and use of data); (ii) voids (absence of policy and therefore data); and (ii) waste in the production of data and formulation of policy. The relationships among these concepts are depicted in Figure 2.3.

EPIC reviews all policy documents related to one theme with respect to its coherence with a set of agreed principles and intended beneficiaries or target groups. The framework thus maps out the social, economic, environmental, and institutional dimensions of every issue that requires policy action. It also identifies target groups that will benefit from policy implementation and develops indicators for the key issues identified. EPIC produces a diverse set of outputs that include indicators needed for the current policies, data gaps for monitoring agreed policies, new agreements on policy priorities, and inputs to future work for filling the current policy void. The three tools featured in this section are already being used in several regions, including Asia and the Pacific. Information on other tools that can be used for addressing SDG connections and enhancing policy and institutional coherence were presented at a learning session at the 2018 High-Level Political Forum. [30]

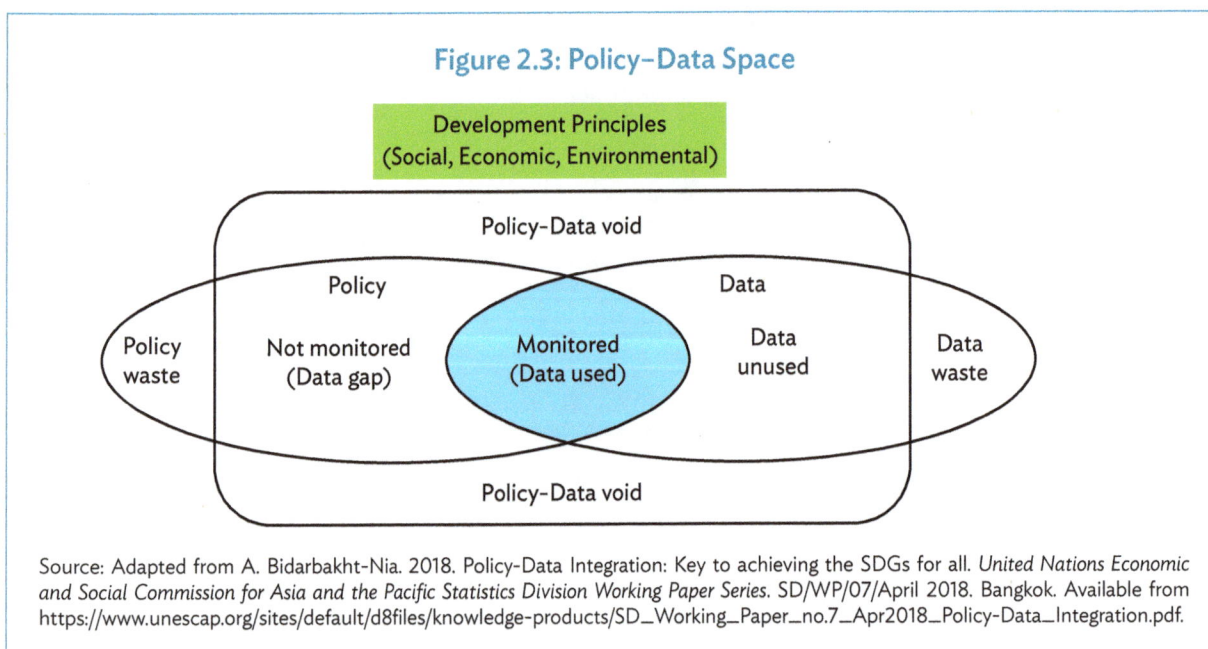

Figure 2.3: Policy–Data Space

Source: Adapted from A. Bidarbakht-Nia. 2018. Policy-Data Integration: Key to achieving the SDGs for all. *United Nations Economic and Social Commission for Asia and the Pacific Statistics Division Working Paper Series.* SD/WP/07/April 2018. Bangkok. Available from https://www.unescap.org/sites/default/d8files/knowledge-products/SD_Working_Paper_no.7_Apr2018_Policy-Data_Integration.pdf.

---

29   A. Bidarbakht-Nia, C. Ryan, and S. Serrao. 2019. Every Policy Is Connected (EPIC): A generic tool for policy-data integration. *UN ESCAP Statistics Division Working Paper Series.* SD/WP/09/September 2019. Bangkok. https://www.unescap.org/sites/default/d8files/knowledge-products/SD_Working_Paper_no.9_Sep2019_EPIC_tool.pdf.

30   HLPF. 2018. Summary of Learning Session at 2018 High-Level Political Forum. New York. 11 July. *Supporting an integrated implementation of the SDGs: Tools for addressing SDG connections and enhancing policy and institutional coherence.*

Advanced Data Planning Tool (ADAPT)

The Partnership in Statistics for Development in the 21st Century (PARIS21) developed a complementary policy–data tool called ADAPT, which examines the cost of development of specific SDG indicators (Figure 2.4).[31] This is an online tool meant specifically for national SDG managers. ADAPT goes beyond currently available data and begins by setting policy targets. The tool supports the process of indicator development when there is agreement on policy targets. If data are not available, the tool helps estimate the costs of compilation of the SDG indicator(s). In the context of the policy–data nexus for SDG indicators, ADAPT can help by presenting reports (with charts and tables) on (i) the policy relevance of applicable SDG indicators, (ii) the availability of applicable SDG indicators, (iii) available SDG indicators by prevailing data sources, (iv) levels of dependency on external technical and financial assistance for available SDG indicators, and (v) the feasibility to compile and produce applicable but unavailable SDG indicators.

ADAPT has a gender module that allows the monitoring of the production of data for gender statistics, particularly those linked to relevant global commitments and national policies. The module assists users in tagging indicators as gender-relevant according to national and global priorities. Reports that can be produced when using the module include indicators that are sex-disaggregated or have been tagged

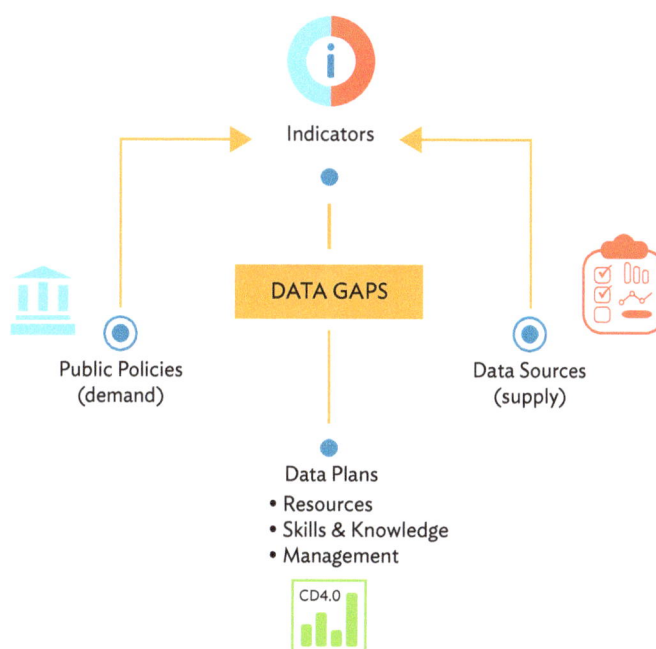

Figure 2.4: The Advanced Data Planning Tool (ADAPT): Linking Data and Policies

Note: The ADAPT gender module is further described here: Partnership in Statistics for Development in the 21st Century (PARIS21). *ADAPT Gender Module.* https://paris21.org/sites/default/files/inline-files/Gender_ADAPT_2pp_A5.pdf.

Source: Adapted from PARIS21. ADAPT. Available at https://paris21.org/advanced-data-planning-tool-adapt.

---

[31]   PARIS21. ADAPT. https://paris21.org/advanced-data-planning-tool-adapt.

as gender-relevant across national and global policies, such as the 54 SDG gender-specific indicators identified by the UN Entity for Gender Equality and the Empowerment of Women (UN Women) and the 52 quantitative indicators of the Minimum Set of Gender Indicators determined by the Inter-agency and Expert Group on Gender Statistics.

The national statistics offices (NSOs) of Cambodia, Cameroon, Equatorial Guinea, Maldives, Mongolia, the Philippines, Rwanda, and Tanzania, among others, have made use of ADAPT. The tool was also introduced in 2018 across 20 countries supported by the United Nations Statistics Division (UNSD) and the Government of the United Kingdom.[32]

StaTact

StaTact was developed by the UN Institute for Training and Research and the UN Statistics Division (UNSD) to enable countries to address measurement gaps that impede monitoring national policies, and to leverage the 2030 Agenda for Sustainable Development to help resolve problems tactically.[33] It provides an analytical framework and a multi-stakeholder methodology that facilitates commitment and collaboration of a team of national experts from NSOs, concerned ministries, and other members of the data community (including nontraditional data sources) to jointly design a short-term action plan that addresses institutional impediments to data collection, production, and utilization. The objective is to help stakeholders achieve their goals in a cost-effective manner within one year of implementation of the plan.

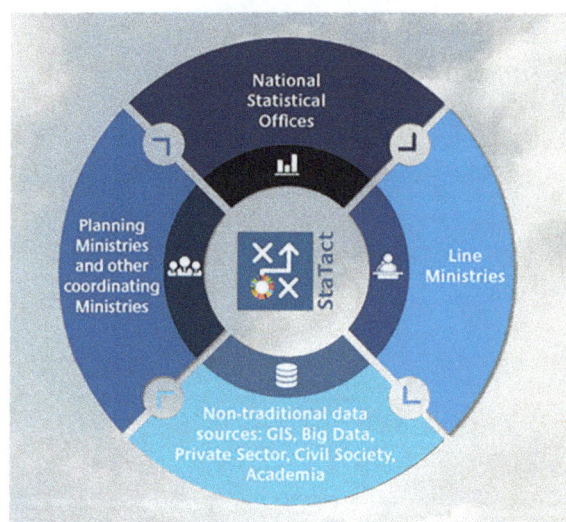

Figure 2.5: StaTact

Source: Available from StaTact. About StaTact. Adapted from https://statact.unitar.org/en/about-statact.

After having been used by 15 pilot countries (primarily African and Asian least developed countries) and 1 small island development state in 2018, StaTact moved online in early 2019 and has been used by 13 small island developing states.

---

[32] UN Department of Economic and Social Affairs. *Enhancing national statistical capacity to measure, monitor, assess and report on progress on achieving post-2015 goals and targets for sustainable development.* https://www.un.org/development/desa/capacity-development/projects/project/statistical-capacity-for-progress-on-sdgs/.

[33] StaTact. About StaTact. https://statact.unitar.org/en/about-statact.

Resources

Recommended Reading

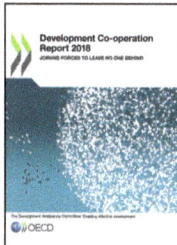

Organisation for Economic Co-operation and Development. 2018. *Development Co-operation Report 2018: Joining Forces to Leave No One Behind.* Paris: OECD Publishing. https://www.oecd-ilibrary.org/development/development-co-operation-report-2018_dcr-2018-en.

Part I of the report provides evidence of why leave no one behind matters along with data and analysis on what it means to be left behind. Chapters in this part zoom in on eight critical issues that need to be tackled to achieve the Sustainable Development Goals (SDGs) for all: (i) ending extreme poverty in countries most in need, (ii) tackling rising income inequality, (iii) addressing fragility, (iv) enabling inclusive governance, (v) taking climate action, (vi) making progress toward gender equality and women's economic empowerment, (vii) including the world's 1.2 billion young people, and (viii) ensuring persons with disabilities are no longer left behind.

Part II investigates leaving no one behind in practice. Chapters in this part shed light on the potential impact of more integrated policies, budgets and programs across sectors and between levels of government in reaching the most vulnerable. Achieving the SDGs for all relies on data and diagnostics that count everyone and are disaggregated by factors like income, sex and gender, geography, age, and disability.

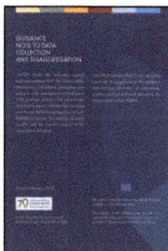

United Nations Office of the High Commissioner for Human Rights. 2018. *A Human Rights-Based Approach to Data: Leaving No One Behind in the 2030 Agenda for Sustainable Development—Guidance Note to Data Collection and Disaggregation.* Geneva. https://www.ohchr.org/Documents/Issues/HRIndicators/GuidanceNoteon ApproachtoData.pdf.

This publication provides detailed discussions and recommendations and good practices on a human rights-based approach to data.

STRENGTHS, POTENTIALS, AND LIMITATIONS OF THE SOURCES OF DISAGGREGATED DATA

Overview

Before embarking on a disaggregation exercise, there are many issues to consider. This includes specific challenges for different data sources. For example, as large sample sizes are needed for disaggregation it can be expensive to collect the data through household surveys. The International Organization for Migration's Global Migration Data Analysis Centre conducted a pilot study on disaggregating Sustainable Development Goal (SDG) indicators by migratory status based on harmonized census data for 73 countries.[34] However, census data often takes years to be released before they can be analyzed. As a result, national statistics offices (NSOs) may explore the potential of administrative data sources or census micro-data for SDG data.

One of the challenges in defining disaggregation categories is that some important concepts relevant to disaggregation lack internationally agreed definitions. Further, there are important considerations beyond data collection. For example, there may be a need for specialized awareness-raising in NSOs on the importance of disaggregation in the first place, or for tailored approaches to disseminate disaggregated data to policy makers in the right ministries.

This chapter looks at main sources of disaggregated data, illustrating how they have been successfully used, the inherent limitations of the sources, how countries are applying innovations to better tap their potential for meeting disaggregation requirements for SDG indicators, and the current capacity limitations.

3.1 Census

Two approaches to data collection that national statistical systems have traditionally relied on are censuses and sample surveys. A census is generally a study of every unit (everyone or everything) in a specified population. A census is often described as a complete enumeration or a complete count of population units. In a sample survey, on the other hand, data are collected from a part (sample) of the total population. Both approaches provide data that are used to draw conclusions about the whole population. This section looks at censuses as sources of disaggregated data. The main types of censuses (differentiated by the units of observation) are a population and housing census, a business and industry census, and an agriculture census.

---

[34] International Organization for Migration. 2018. *A pilot study on disaggregating SDG indicators by migratory status*. Geneva. https://publications.iom.int/system/files/pdf/a_pilot_study_on_disaggregating_sdg_indicators.pdf.

Censuses provide disaggregated data in several ways:

(i)   A population and housing census can provide data to calculate directly indicators on the topics it covers. Typically, censuses cover the following disaggregation dimensions: sex/gender, age, ethnicity/race, disability status, migrant status, education level, and geographic location (e.g., administrative or subnational areas, urban/rural).

(ii)   Censuses can serve as a sample frame for surveys, providing the reference population for the special/vulnerable population groups. For example, censuses where identification of disability status of persons is a data item can be used to construct sampling frames for disability surveys.

(iii)   Censuses can be used as inputs for small area estimation modeling to produce disaggregated data.

(iv)   Censuses can be used for geospatial data analysis.

Potential

Innovations to censuses and surveys to address SDG needs are exemplified in the Food and Agriculture Organization (FAO) of the United Nations (UN) initiatives described in Box 3.1.

Box 3.1: What's New in Data Collection for the Sustainable Development Goals in Agricultural Censuses and Surveys?

The Food and Agriculture Organization of the United Nations (FAO) World Programme for the Census of Agriculture provides assistance and guidance to countries to conduct national agricultural censuses. Collected data provide an overview of the state of a country's agriculture sector, including size of holdings, land tenure, land use, area harvested, irrigation, livestock, labor, and other agricultural inputs. This information is essential in agricultural planning and policy making, research and development, and tracking the impact of agriculture on the environment.

For this 2020 round, FAO has developed a new set of guidelines that entail a number of developments considering the evolving nature of data use and collection. New data collection technologies such as computer-assisted personal interviewing have been added to enhance data quality and substantially reduce the time lag between data collection and analysis. The guidelines also stress the use of web-based data (e.g., tables, graphs, maps) and interactive outputs, and access to anonymized micro-data, as new prospects for census dissemination. Data domains have been added and/or proposed, such as fisheries and greenhouse gas emissions, to help in monitoring the gains of the Sustainable Development Goals (SDGs). There is also a renewed approach among the new methodologies introduced for assessing food security by reviewing the severity of food insecurity as confronted by individuals in the population. For this round, the World Programme for the Census of Agriculture has also improved the process for measuring the distribution of managerial decisions and for the collection of sex-disaggregated data started the identification of ownership within the household.[a] Recent global initiatives that seek to address the lack of sex-disaggregated data in agricultural censuses and surveys include the FAO and World Bank Global Strategy to Improve Agricultural and Rural Statistics; the Evidence on Data and Gender Equality project, which has worked with FAO on clear recommendations for agricultural censuses to include

continued on next page

Box 3.1 *continued*

sex-disaggregated data on land ownership; and a FAO report and guide, the Agri-Gender Statistics Toolkit, on integrating gender in agricultural surveys.[b] The adoption of the SDGs starting in 2015 and efforts of international agencies to address gender data gaps in agriculture through enhancements of household surveys directed at the household and agricultural landholding levels benefited the availability of gender-disaggregated data in household surveys. The World Bank's Living Standards Measurement Study–Integrated Surveys on Agriculture for instance, have been frequently used in recent research of women's and men's outcomes in agriculture in sub-Saharan Africa. The Global Environment Facility's Integrated Approach on Food Security is another project-specific household survey, which explores how to further establish sex-disaggregated data in survey modules on agricultural productivity and climate change.[c]

[a] Food and Agriculture Organization of the United Nations. 2015. *World Programme for the Census of Agriculture 2020. Volume 1. Programme, concepts, and definitions.* https://ec.europa.eu/eurostat/ramon/statmanuals/files/world_census_agri_2020_EN.pdf.

[b] Food and Agriculture Organization of the United Nations. 2016. *Agri-Gender Statistics Toolkit.* Ankara. http://www.fao.org/3/i5769e/i5769e.pdf.

[c] Food and Agriculture Organization of the United Nations. 2019. *Integrated Approach Program on Food Security.* https://www.thegef.org/project/food-iap-fostering-sustainability-and-resilience-food-security-sub-saharan-africa-integrated.

For most countries, the population census is the only source that produces information on population count and its distributions. The *Technical Report: Measuring Sustainable Development Goals Indicators Through Population and Housing Censuses and Civil Registration and Vital Statistics Data,* concludes that for about 40% of the SDGs indicators which are related to population, the census can provide reliable data for denominators, either directly or through the population projections based on census data.[35] It identifies 12 SDG indicators for which the population census is the most obvious source for disaggregation variables and 10 additional indicators for which census data can be used for proxy estimation. In particular, census data provide information on disability and migratory status.

A new methodology to generate spatially disaggregated population estimates through a hybrid census is described in Box 3.2.

Limitations

Censuses are conducted only every 5 or 10 years. As direct sources of data, these provide at most only two data points for the census indicators. However, census data have longer-term value as bases for population projections and sampling frames; when integrated with other data such as surveys and administrative data, these data are invaluable.

[35] UNSD. 2020. *Technical Report: Measuring Sustainable Development Goals Indicators Through Population and Housing Censuses and Civil Registration and Vital Statistics Data.* https://www.unescap.org/sites/default/files/Technical_report_Workshop_SDG_PHC_CRVS_27-30Oct_and_2-6Nov2020.pdf.

Box 3.2: New Methodology: A Hybrid Census to Generate Spatially Disaggregated Population Estimates[a]

Within the 2030 Agenda for Sustainable Development, the growing requirement for spatially disaggregated population data has triggered the exploration of new data sources at different geographical scales and time periods, especially in highly stressed countries and countries without a recent population census. The developments on the use of detailed available satellite imagery, geo-positioning tools for field surveys, statistical methods, and computational power are allowing the enhancement and use of methods that can estimate more granular population scales across countries, in cases where population and housing census cannot be conducted.[b]

The goal of a hybrid census is to produce population estimates for small areas, or uniform, detailed grids in the absence of a traditional national census. Hybrid censuses rely on complete counts of population within small, defined areas, through "micro-census surveys". These can be selected based on areas of interest and data can be gathered relatively faster at much lower cost compared to a full census. For areas not sampled, statistical models are used to link the micro-census data to spatial data with full coverage to predict population numbers. Population totals can also be produced for bigger administrative units or for the national level through aggregation.[c]

This approach cannot fully replace the data produced by a traditional population and housing census. However, in the absence of a census data from conventional sources due to conflict or other concerns, the hybrid approach can generate population estimates for small areas.[d]

[a] UN Population Fund. 2017. *New Methodology: a hybrid census to generate spatially disaggregated population estimates—Technical Brief.* https://www.unfpa.org/sites/default/files/resource-pdf/Hybrid_Census_Brief_v9.pdf.

[b] N. A. Wardrop, W. C. Jochem, T. J. Bird, H. R. Chamberlain, D. Clarke, D. Kerr, L. Bengtsson, S. Juran, V. Seaman, and A. J. Tatem. 2018. *Spatially disaggregated population estimates in the absence of national population and housing census data.* Proceedings of the National Academy of Sciences Apr 2018, 115 (14) 3529-3537. https://www.pnas.org/content/115/14/3529.

[c] Geo-referenced Infrastructure and Demographic Data for Development. 2020. *High resolution population estimates.* https://grid3.org/solution/high-resolution-population-estimates.

[d] B. Hellali. 2018. *Hybrid census to generate spatially-disaggregated population estimates.* https://unstats.un.org/unsd/undataforum/blog/hybrid-census-to-generate-spatially-disaggregated-population-estimates/.

3.2   Sample Surveys

A total of 80 indicators, distributed across 13 SDGs, are being or could be sourced from household surveys. About 70% of the indicators calculated from household survey data have a requirement of at least one level of disaggregation, supporting the overall goal of "leave no one behind" (LNOB). Of 80 indicators, 37 have age as a minimum disaggregation dimension, followed by sex (32), disability (14), and income (8). Household surveys offer the potential to help achieve the minimum disaggregation requirements of the SDG global indicator framework since they cover a wide range of topics by design.

Some of the major internationally comparable household surveys include (i) the Demographic Health Surveys (DHS) Program, funded by the United States Agency for International Development; (ii) the Multiple Indicator Cluster Surveys (MICS), overseen by the United Nations Children's Fund (UNICEF); and (iii) the LSMS surveys, supported by the World Bank. These household surveys are usually conducted every 3 to 5 years.[36]

Potential

Household survey data provide numerous disaggregation possibilities, of which many are not yet fully exploited. Household surveys offer flexibility in the range of disaggregation dimensions that are covered through sampling approaches and the questions asked. Although household surveys are not well suited to generate spatial disaggregates at lower administrative levels, basic disaggregates such as place of residence, sex, wealth status, and age are usually available. However, innovative approaches such as combinations of these (e.g., poor in urban areas, young women) or the ability to generate indicators for specific subgroups across many dimensions (e.g., multidimensional poverty) lend more analytical power to the data.

Apart from basic disaggregates, household survey data provide numerous other disaggregates and outcomes that other data systems do not have; household surveys can expand the breadth of SDG indicators covered with ease compared to administrative systems, which collect small numbers of indicators. Despite this, countries and survey programs do not typically exploit the full potential of micro-data. Future work must ensure that adequate further analysis frameworks and tools are developed to better understand the data collected.

Limitations

Sample Sizes and Reliability

A survey that is intended to compile a (socioeconomic) development indicator typically comprises a sample size that is large enough to provide nationally representative estimates. The sample size generally also provides estimates that fall within tolerable levels of reliability when further disaggregating indicators by broad domains such as states, regions, or provinces. However, the high cost of conducting surveys prevents a data collection agency from increasing the sample size that would produce reliable estimates at more granular levels, such as municipalities and villages.

To substantiate this argument, consider a hypothetical population comprising 20 million households across 17 regions and 85 provinces. Furthermore, suppose the objective is to estimate a parameter of interest (expressed as a ratio) with a margin of error of 0.05 and a 95% confidence level based on different levels of disaggregation. If one employs simple random sampling, it requires data collection from about 6,800 households to be able to produce a nationally representative estimate that meets the pre-specified accuracy levels. If, however, the objective is to provide regionally representative estimates, wherein each estimator meets the pre-specified accuracy thresholds, one needs to sample about 115,000 households. The required sample size further increases to 575,000 households to produce provincially representative estimates.

---

[36] DHS Program. https://dhsprogram.com; MICS. http://mics.unicef.org; and LSMS. https://www.worldbank.org/en/programs/lsms.

Figure 3.1: Recommended Sample Size for Different Levels of Geographic Disaggregation

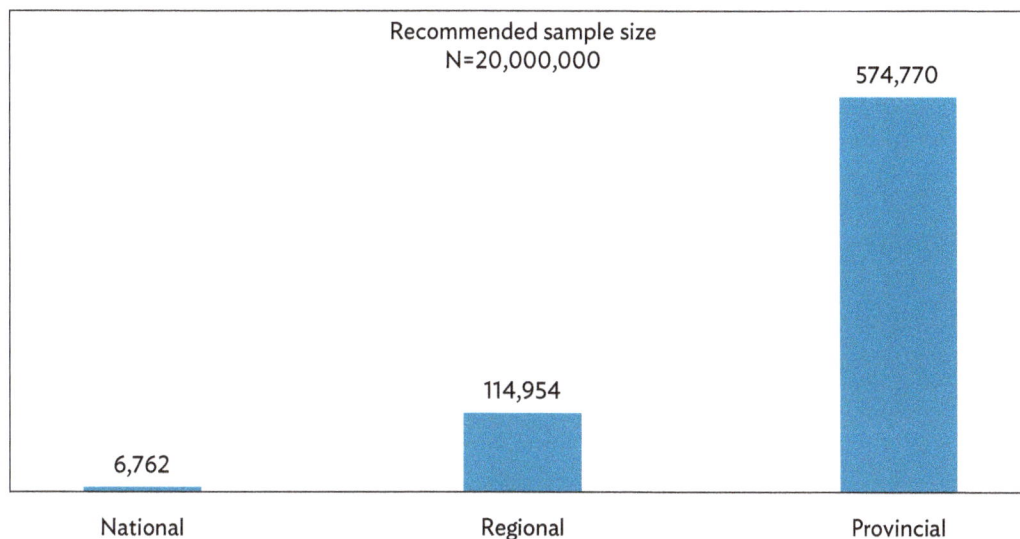

Recommended sample size
N=20,000,000

National	6,762
Regional	114,954
Provincial	574,770

Source: Adapted from Asian Development Bank. 2020. *Introduction to Small Area Estimation Techniques: A Practical Guide for National Statistics Offices.* Manila. Available from https://www.adb.org/sites/default/files/publication/609476/small-area-estimation-guide-nsos.pdf.

Figure 3.1 highlights that to produce granular survey estimates, increasing the survey's sample size is ideal as long as financial and technical resources are not an issue. However, this is not usually true for many NSOs or data collection agencies that conduct such surveys. Often, they are constrained by limited budgets and resources, which affects collection of data on migrants, the elderly, or persons with disabilities.

Sample surveys, which have been typically designed to yield reliable estimates up to the national or regional levels given the costs of data collection, will need increased sample sizes to allow the generation of reliable data for specific sectors of the population, such as migrants, the elderly, or the disabled. Larger sample sizes require additional financial costs.

Bias Because of Underreporting on Sensitive Topics

The sensitivity of some SDG indicators, such as indicators pertaining to violence against women and children or maternal death, could lead family members to underreport these, particularly in household surveys. Further, both maternal mortality and violence against women and children may be relatively rare. A household survey would thus find few respondents who have experienced violence against women and children or a maternal death (or who have a relative who died of pregnancy-related causes) in their household. The margin of error attached to these estimates of the proportion of households that have experienced violence against women and children and maternal mortality rate is very large.

Omissions

In some cases, disaggregated data may not be available from traditional data sources because requisite basic data have not been collected. Several household surveys, for instance, omit by design some persons in the population: those who are homeless, or who sleep in their workplaces, which are not enumerated as dwellings; those who are in institutions, including refugee camps; and those from nomadic populations. In addition, household surveys typically do not adequately cover those who reside in areas with security risks or that are remotely accessible. The customary length of a sample survey and the need to maintain confidentiality for the collection of culturally sensitive data (e.g., ethnicity data) have also constrained production of disaggregated data.

Adjustments in survey designs should be made, or special surveys targeting these omitted populations or undercounted groups in traditional surveys need to be carried out, since these population groups are likely marginalized and, in addition, are invisible to current measurement systems.

3.3   Administrative Reporting Systems

Administrative reporting systems data come from registers of records such as hospital or school records. These are cheaper to collect than survey data, but coverage in many countries is incomplete and data quality can be problematic, as data are not usually designed for statistical purposes.

An important type of administrative data is from the civil registration system, which exists for the legal recording of vital events (such as births, marriages, and deaths) of the population on a continuous basis.

Potential

NSOs and other data producers in government used to generate statistics only from censuses and sample surveys, which were designed specifically for statistical purposes. Data sources subsequently expanded to administrative reporting systems as national statistical systems (NSSs) came under pressure to improve the efficiency of the statistical production process by saving on costs and staff resources. At the same time, there was growing demand to reduce the burden on respondents in sample surveys and censuses. While administrative-based data are rarely direct substitutes for data collected from censuses and sample surveys, this type of data offers possibilities for reducing the cost in statistics generation and the burden on respondents.

Limitations

Data on maternal mortality ratios can be alternatively and ideally sourced from vital registration systems, but, across many countries, these data systems do not have full coverage, especially on deaths. There may be incentives to have births registered in some countries. Deaths can be seriously underreported and information on causes of death, as collected from death registration systems or even medical certifications, may also be misreported.

3.4   Small Area Estimation

Strengths

Sample surveys are designed to produce reliable statistics at a given level of aggregation defined by sampling domains, generally geographical or socioeconomic subgroups of the population. This is achieved by, among other design considerations, determining the sample size required to produce reliable estimates for the specified aggregation level. However, there is often a subsequent demand for estimates at a more disaggregated level. Producing statistical estimates for more disaggregated levels than were originally planned from survey data without increasing the survey sample size (and hence the cost of data collection) is the objective of small area estimation (SAE).

A *"small area"* may refer to a *geographic area*, which is more disaggregated than the geographic domain for which the survey is originally designed to provide reliable estimates. Going back to the example in Section 3.2 on the hypothetical population of 20 million households distributed among 85 provinces within 17 regions, regions and provinces could be both considered as small areas.

In addition, the term *"small area"* may refer to *socioeconomic subgroups*, such as age, sex, and/or ethnic group of persons, and the vulnerable groups targeted by the 2030 Agenda.

SAE is a class of statistical techniques anchored on the notion of combining multiple data sources and capitalizing on the strengths of each source. Consider, for example, the strengths of a survey and those of a census. Compared to a census, a survey is a more flexible data-collection vehicle in terms of the range of information it can collect. In contrast, a census typically collects less detailed information. But there is also a flipside when conducting surveys, as survey estimates are subject to margins of error that could be inflated if the sample size is too small. SAE techniques include ones that combine (i) a survey and a census to capitalize on the wide range or detailed information that a survey collects and (ii) the wide coverage a census data set affords. In this context, census data are referred to as "auxiliary data." In addition to census data, data from administrative reporting systems provide auxiliary data for SAE.

There is a wide range of SAE techniques, and the choice usually depends on what is being estimated, what types of auxiliary data sources are available, and the desired level of disaggregation. Three general approaches are (i) direct survey estimation, (ii) SAE using auxiliary information, and (iii) SAE using regression-based models.[37] Commonly used methods include broad area ratio estimation, calibration methods, weight reallocation, empirical best linear unbiased prediction, and other regression-based methods. Figure 3.2 provides a relationship diagram of these methods.

SAE techniques can be applied to further disaggregate SDG indicators that are traditionally compiled from surveys. Some illustrations on poverty, unemployment, and health indicators are provided in Boxes 3.3, 3.4, and 3.5.

---

[37] For detailed discussion on these techniques, see ADB. 2020. *Introduction to Small Area Estimation Techniques: A Practical Guide for National Statistical Offices*. Manila. https://www.adb.org/sites/default/files/publication/609476/small-area-estimation-guide-nsos.pdf.

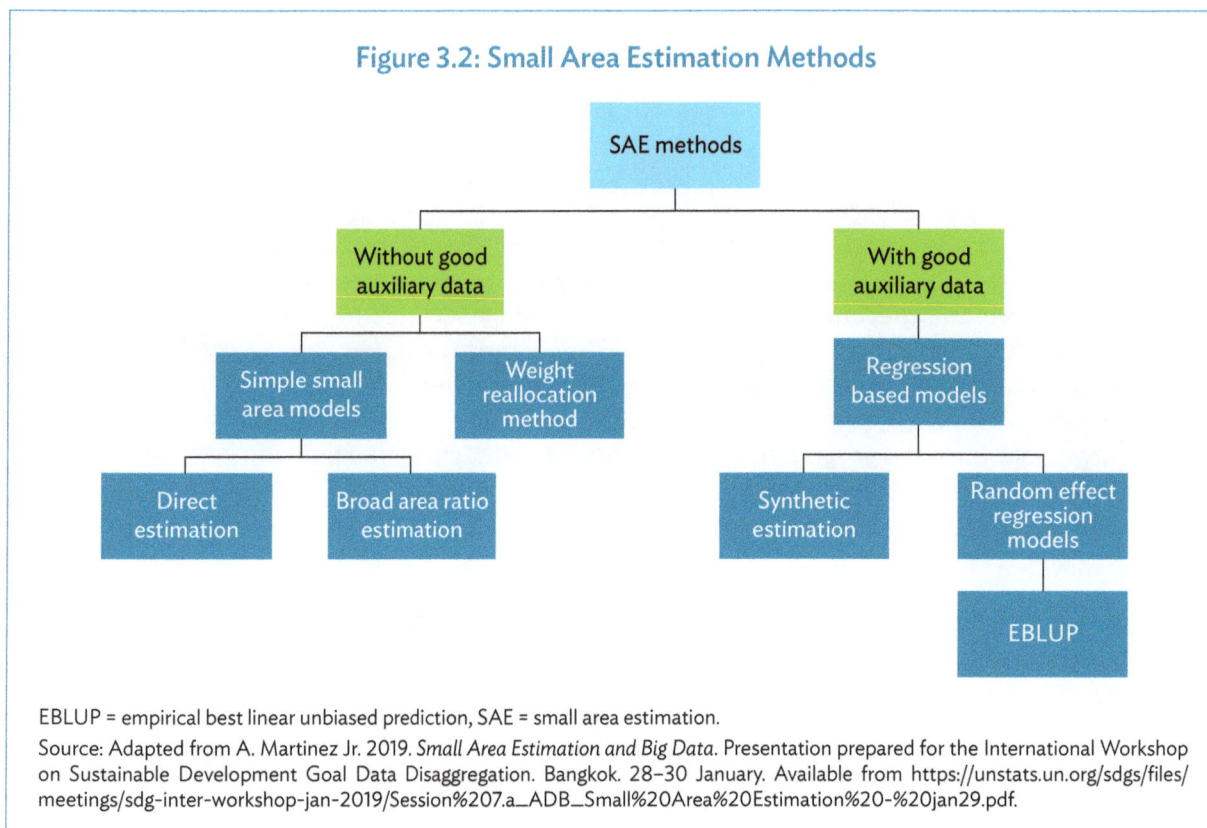

Figure 3.2: Small Area Estimation Methods

EBLUP = empirical best linear unbiased prediction, SAE = small area estimation.
Source: Adapted from A. Martinez Jr. 2019. *Small Area Estimation and Big Data*. Presentation prepared for the International Workshop on Sustainable Development Goal Data Disaggregation. Bangkok. 28–30 January. Available from https://unstats.un.org/sdgs/files/meetings/sdg-inter-workshop-jan-2019/Session%207.a_ADB_Small%20Area%20Estimation%20-%20jan29.pdf.

Poverty-Related Indicators

A relatively well-developed application is the disaggregation of **poverty-related indicators**. For instance, a household income and expenditure survey or a living standards survey is used to compile statistics on people living below a national or international poverty line. Like many household surveys, a typical household income and expenditure survey or a living standards survey has sample sizes large enough to provide reliable estimates when poverty statistics are summarized by population groups (e.g., gender, age, occupation of an individual or household head) at the national or regional level, but not necessarily to provide reliable estimates when disaggregated at finer levels. One of the commonly used SAE techniques for poverty estimation is the *empirical best linear unbiased prediction* (EBLUP) which is described in Box 3.3.

Box 3.3: How to Estimate the Empirical Best Linear Unbiased Prediction (EBLUP)

First, one calculates poverty statistics for the desired set of small areas, using data from surveys. Second, one finds potential covariates, available at the small area level, for the calculated poverty statistics from auxiliary data. Third, the survey-based poverty statistics compiled at the small area level are regressed on the potential covariates. Lastly, the weighted average of the poverty statistics compiled in the first step and predicted poverty statistics from the third step is taken, where the weights are inversely proportional to the variance of the model error and sampling error. Such approach is feasible when the following two criteria are met: (i) all small areas are represented in the survey and (ii) there are auxiliary data available at the desired small area level that are correlated with the poverty indicator being estimated.

Source: ADB. 2020. *Introduction to Small Area Estimation Techniques: A Practical Guide for National Statistics Offices.* Manila. https://www.adb.org/sites/default/files/publication/609476/small-area-estimation-guide-nsos.pdf.

If any of the criteria for estimating the empirical best linear unbiased prediction are not met, an alternative is the poverty mapping method popularized by the World Bank, which is also referred to as the Elbers, Lanjouw, and Lanjouw method. The method entails integrating income or expenditure data from household income and expenditure surveys or living standards surveys with auxiliary data from population censuses (ideally collected in the same year). It employs the survey data to build an econometric model by regressing the household-level data on income or expenditure collected from surveys with income correlates that are both available from surveys and censuses. The parameter coefficients derived from the econometric model are then applied to the census values of the income correlates. This method yields income or expenditure predictions for every unit in the census data.

Box 3.4: Poverty Mapping

Uganda (2018). The Uganda Bureau of Statistics, United Nations Children's Fund (UNICEF), and the World Bank created new poverty maps at the sub-county level based on the Elbers, Lanjouw, and Lanjouw method. The maps include child poverty estimates across all geographic regions. The small area estimation (SAE) estimates were based on the 2012–2013 Uganda national household survey and the 2014 national population and housing census.[a]

[a] The methodology, mapping exercise and validation and results are presented at World Bank, Uganda Bureau of Statistics, and UNICEF. 2018. *Poverty Maps of Uganda: Mapping the Spatial Distribution of Poor Households Based on Data from the 2012/13 Uganda National Household Survey and the 2014 National Housing and Population Census—Technical Report.* http://documents1.worldbank.org/curated/en/456801530034180435/pdf/Poverty-Maps-Report.pdf.

Unemployment Rates

> ### Box 3.5: Small Area Estimation Applied to Unemployment Rates in Indonesia (2015)
>
> The National Labor Force Survey of Indonesia is conducted based on a quarterly rotating panel survey. Because groups differ according to their time in panel and observation strategy, it leads to bias. In addition, sample size is not adequate to obtain reliable direct estimates of indicators at the district level (small area). In 2015, a small area estimation (SAE) model that accommodated the bias component because of the rotation was applied, but it assumed the effect over time followed a random walk process, so it was necessary to develop a model that is more general. Estimates from an SAE model for the rotation group level, combined with the time-series multilevel model and the Rao-Yu model, have produced data to estimate a quarterly unemployment rate at the district level.[a]
>
> ---
>
> [a] The Rao-Yu model is applied to both cross-sectional and time series data that involved the use of autocorrelated random effects and sampling errors for small area estimation.
>
> Source: S. Muchlisoh et al. 2015. Estimation of unemployment rate using small area estimation model based on a rotating panel national labor force survey. *Indonesian Journal of Statistics*. 20 (2). pp. 1–4. http://journal.ipb.ac.id/index.php/statistika/article/download/16755/12206.

Health-Related Indicators

SAE is also used to compile more disaggregated data on **health indicators** compiled through surveys. For example, in addition to providing disaggregated data on income- or expenditure-based indicators like poverty and inequality, the Elbers, Lanjouw, and Lanjouw method has been used to produce disaggregated data on non-income indicators like stunting and wasting, as well as health and disease maps, in a number of countries.[38] In the United States, the SAE technique is employed to compile disaggregated data on the prevalence of childhood obesity.[39] Other notable SAE applications include compiling disaggregated data on the number of underweight children aged 0–5 years in municipalities and cities in two different regions, the proportion of underweight children aged 0–5 years, the proportion of Vitamin A-deficient children aged 6 months–5 years, and the prevalence of maternal mortality.[40]

---

[38] R. Van der Weide. 2017. *Poverty Mapping at the World Bank*. Manila. https://psa.gov.ph/content/session-2-1-mr-roy-van-der-weide.

[39] X. Zhang, S. Onufrak, J. Holt, and J. Croft. 2013. *A Multilevel Approach to Estimating Small Area Childhood Obesity Prevalence at the Census Block-Group Level*. Prev Chronic Dis 2013;10:120252. https://www.cdc.gov/pcd/issues/2013/12_0252.htm.

[40] S.B. Aracid. 2014. *Indirect Estimates of the City and Municipality Level Counts of Underweight Children Aged 0–5 Years in MIMAROPA Region*. Unpublished Undergraduate Special Problem, Institute of Statistics. University of the Philippines, Los Baños; C.E.N. Relente. 2010. *Municipal and City Level Estimation of the Number of Underweight 0-5-Year-Old Children in Bicol Region*. Unpublished Undergraduate Special Problem, Institute of Statistics. University of the Philippines, Los Baños; R.L. Arlan. 2016. *Small Area Estimation of the City and Municipal Level Proportion of 0-5-Year-Old Underweight Children in the Philippines*. Unpublished Master's Thesis, University of the Philippines, Los Baños; L.P.D. Abitona. 2011. *Provincial Level Estimation of the Proportion of Vitamin A Deficient Children Aged 6 Months to 5 Years in the Philippines*. Unpublished Master's Thesis, University of the Philippines, Los Baños; and I.D.P. Nuestro. 2014. *Municipal and City Level Estimation of the Total Number of Maternal Deaths in MIMAROPA*. Unpublished Undergraduate Special Problem, Institute of Statistics. University of the Philippines, Los Baños.

Potential

Overall, SAE could be a potentially more cost-effective analytical tool for providing disaggregated estimates for a wide range of SDG indicators that are traditionally compiled from surveys alone. However, SAE requires the availability of auxiliary data, and several techniques employ normative assumptions, the validity of which need to be carefully examined.

Thus, before one embarks on an SAE exercise, it is important to have clarity on what type of disaggregated data are needed, and why such type of data is needed—what are the key policies, funding decisions, or questions that disaggregated statistics can address? SAE should be done when there is a valid need for disaggregated statistics but no other proxy data at the small area level are available for use in policy making and program planning. In some instances, volumes of data are readily available, yet remain untapped. In relation to the SDG data requirements for disaggregated indicators, this information and these conditions on small area estimation are articulated in the global SDG commitments, but some work still needs to be done at the national level.

Limitations

Implementing SAE does not always provide reliable estimates at all desired levels of disaggregation. In some instances, data producers publish estimates calculated directly from surveys at the small area level, but with notes or caveats stating that caution should be taken when examining small areas for which reliability of survey estimates fall below a pre-specified threshold. On the other hand, the application of SAE becomes more compelling when many units of the desired level of disaggregation have direct survey estimates falling below a pre-specified reliability threshold.

National statistical surveys require considerable financial and technical resources, and SAE is regarded as a more cost-efficient tool compared to increasing the sample size of surveys. Because different stakeholders may need varying levels of disaggregation, it is important to identify whose data needs can be addressed most efficiently by conducting SAE through consultations. SAE is not a solution that can address every user's disaggregated data requirements; thus, consultation is a good opportunity to communicate the limitations of SAE to target users.

In the context of SDG monitoring, it is important to note that SAE is not a silver bullet that can address all of the disaggregated data requirements. SAE techniques that start with sample survey data would thus not be relevant for indicators that are not derived from surveys. There are also instances when fundamental issues such as the absence of consistent conceptual definitions, and others remain unresolved, which prevents the compilation of disaggregated data.

Recommended Reading

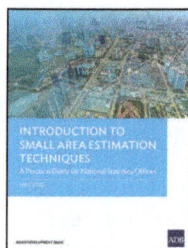

Asian Development Bank. 2020. *Introduction to Small Area Estimation Techniques: A Practical Guide for National Statistics Offices.* Manila. https://www.adb.org/sites/default/files/publication/609476/small-area-estimation-guide-nsos.pdf.

This guide provides an introduction to basic small area estimation (SAE) techniques and describes the implementation of these techniques using R software.

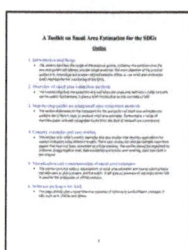

A Toolkit on Small Area Estimation for the SDGs. https://unstats.un.org/iswghs/task-forces/task-forces-round2/.

The Joint Intersecretariat Working Group on Household Surveys and the Inter-agency Expert Group on Sustainable Development Goal Indicators (IAEG-SDGs) Task Force on Small Area Estimates led by the United Nations Statistics Division (UNSD) and members from national statistics offices (NSOs), international agencies, academia, and nongovernment organizations are developing a toolkit on small area estimation (SAE) for the Sustainable Development Goals (SDGs). The toolkit includes an overview of SAE methods, step-by-step guide on using SAE methods, country examples and case studies, visualization and communication of SAEs, and software packages for SAE. The tentative title of the toolkit is "SAE4SDG".

3.5   Big Data, Geospatial Data, and Others

"Big data," referred to as digital footprints, are data that are too large and complex for processing by traditional database management tools, offer possibilities to address SDG data disaggregation gaps or to complement statistics generated from traditional data sources.[41]

These sources can be classified as shown in Table 3.1.[42]

---

[41]   Big data is defined as "an accumulation of data that is too large and complex for processing by traditional database management tools." Merriam-Webster English Dictionary. https://www.merriam-webster.com/dictionary/big%20data.

[42]   UN Statistics Division. 2019. *New data sources for official statistics – access, use and new skills.* Note prepared for the Economic Commission for Europe's Conference of European Statisticians, 67th plenary session. Paris. 26–28 June. https://unece.org/fileadmin/DAM/stats/documents/ece/ces/2019/ECE_CES_2019_41.pdf.

Table 3.1: A Taxonomy of Big Data

Type	Subtype	Examples
Social networks (human-sourced information)	Social networks	Facebook, Twitter, Tumblr
	Blogs and comments	
	Pictures	Instagram, Flickr, Picasa
	Videos	YouTube, TikTok
	Internet searches	
	User-generated maps	
Traditional business systems (process-mediated data)—some sources may fall into the category of "administrative data"[43]	Data produced by public agencies	Medical records
	Data produced by businesses	Commercial transactions: scanner data
		Banking and/or stock records
		e-commerce
		Credit cards
Internet of things (machine-generated data)	Data from sensors	Fixed sensors: home automation, weather/pollution sensors, traffic sensors or webcams, security or surveillance videos
		Mobile sensors (tracking): mobile phone location, cars, satellite images
	Data from computer systems	Logs, web logs

Source: UN Statistics Division. 2019. *New data sources for official statistics – access, use and new skills.* Note prepared for the Economic Commission for Europe's Conference of European Statisticians, 67th plenary session. Paris. 26–28 June. https://unece.org/fileadmin/DAM/stats/documents/ece/ces/2019/ECE_CES_2019_41.pdf.

Big Data Uses for Sustainable Development Goal Indicators Monitoring: Examples

Generally, the use of big data for producing official statistics is still limited, but is expanding.[44] Applications to the production of SDG monitoring indicators drive some of the methodological work in this area. Some examples of ongoing work that facilitate the disaggregation of data for producing SDG indicators are listed in Box 3.6. These examples are not discussed in detail but hyperlinks to available details are provided.

---

[43] Administrative data are "data reported to administrative authorities by individual persons or legal entities for legal compliance or to access government services, data recording decisions made by administrative authorities and data generated by administrative authorities to support planning, implementation, monitoring and evaluation of administrative programmes." UN Statistics Division/DESA. 2018. *Use of administrative data for official statistics: The Global Perspective. Beijing. 26-29 June 2018.* Presentation prepared for the International Workshop on Sustainable Development Indicators. https://unstats.un.org/sdgs/files/meetings/sdg-inter-workshop-june-2018/Day2_Session3_Adm%20Data_UNSD.pdf.

[44] UN. 2020. *Background document for the Note by the Secretary-General transmitting the report of the Global Working Group on Big Data for Official Statistics (E/CN.3/2020/24).* Document prepared for the 51st session of the Statistical Commission. 3–6 March. New York. https://unstats.un.org/unsd/statcom/51st-session/documents/UN_BigData_report_v6.0-E.html.

Box 3.6: Examples of Use of Big Data for Producing Sustainable Development Goal Indicators

Statistics Korea and SK Telecom have launched a data service for population movement between regions, generating statistics on traffic volume by gender and/or age.[a]

Statistics Indonesia and a range of partners are using mobile positioning data to increase coverage and granularity for tourism statistics (Sustainable Development Goal [SDG] targets 8.9 and 12.b) and for commuting and internal migration statistics (SDG targets 10.7 and 11.a).[b]

The Idea Maps Network is integrating four current approaches to slum area mapping and the Flowminder Foundation demonstrated the use of spatial models for slum area mapping.[c]

The Philippines is refining methodology that relates the rural access index (SDG indicator 9.1.1) based on Geographic Information System mapping and software to survey-based poverty estimates.[d]

World Data Lab data models track the SDGs in real time at disaggregated levels, such as through a poverty clock that disaggregates poverty headcount by gender, age, and rural or urban.[e]

[a] Statistics Korea and SK Telecom. 2020. *Mobile Data for Tourism, Migration, Population and Transport in Korea.* Presentation prepared for the 6th International Conference on Big Data for Official Statistics. 31 August–2 September. Virtual conference.https://unstats. un.org/unsd/bigdata/conferences/2020/presentations/day1/session3/1. Dongok Lee.pdf.

[b] Statistics Indonesia. 2020. *Using Big Data for SDGs: Mobile Data for Tourism and Commuting.* Presentation prepared for the prepared for the 6th International Conference on Big Data for Official Statistics. 31 August–2 September. Virtual conference. https://unstats.un.org/unsd/bigdata/conferences/2020/presentations/day1/session3/Use of Mobile Phone for SDGs_rev2.0.pdf.

[c] Idea Maps Network. 2020. *Integrated Deprived Area "Slum" Mapping System.* Presentation prepared for the 6th Conference on Big Data for Official Statistics. 31 August–2 September. Virtual conference. https://unstats.un.org/unsd/bigdata/conferences/2020/ presentations/day2/session6/Ms.%20Dana%20Thompson.pdf; and Flowminder Foundation. 2018. *Spatial Models for Slum Area Mapping.* Presentation prepared for the United Nations Global Geospatial Information Management meeting. 30 November. Nairobi. http://ggim.un.org/meetings/2018-International-Seminar-Kenya/documents/03_thomson_v3.pdf.

[d] Philippine Statistics Authority. 2020. *Relating Rural Access Index and Poverty in the Philippines.* Presentation prepared for the 6th Conference on Big Data for Official Statistics. 31 August–2 September. Virtual conference. https://unstats.un.org/unsd/ bigdata/conferences/2020/presentations/day2/session6/Mr. Justin Angelo.pdf.

[e] World Data Lab. 2019. Presentation prepared for the International Workshop on Data Disaggregation for SDGs. 28-30 January. Bangkok, Thailand. https://unstats.un.org/sdgs/files/meetings/sdg-inter-workshop-jan-2019/Session%207.b_World%20Data%20 Lab.pdf.

The examples provided in Box 3.6 are illustrative of the increasing initiatives in the use of big data for official statistics in general, and for producing disaggregated data needed for SDG monitoring. A methodological challenge is that of providing a "proof of concept" for scalability of some of the results.[45] An example of how one has been developed in relation to producing disaggregated poverty estimates published by the Asian Development Bank (ADB) is described in Box 3.7.[46]

---

[45] A proof of concept is defined as "evidence, typically deriving from an experiment or pilot project, which demonstrates that a design concept, business proposal, etc. is feasible." Oxford English Dictionary. https://www.lexico.com/definition/proof_of_ concept.

[46] Initial results of these studies are in ADB. 2020. *Mapping Poverty through Data Integration and Artificial Intelligence: A Special Supplement of the Key Indicators for Asia and the Pacific 2020.* Manila. https://www.adb.org/sites/default/files/publication/630406/ mapping-poverty-ki2020-supplement.pdf.

Box 3.7: Studies on Scalability—Producing More Disaggregated Poverty Estimates

Under its Data for Development knowledge and support technical assistance project, the Asian Development Bank (ADB) is keeping tabs on relevant initiatives using big data so that countries and their stakeholders can have a more nuanced understanding on the scalability of such initiatives.[a] For example, pilot work in the Philippines and Thailand has combined satellite imagery data with data from censuses and surveys to improve the accuracy and level of disaggregation of small area estimates of poverty incidence. Prior to this pilot work, Thailand and the Philippines combined data from sample surveys with census data through small area estimation (SAE) models to yield more disaggregated poverty estimates.

As discussed in section 3.4, to construct a model of expenditure, income is used (or any other household- or individual-level indicators of welfare) as a function of variables that are common to both the household survey and the census. Estimates from the SAE model, along with census data on the variables that help predict welfare, are used to get predicted values of poverty indicators for every household in the country. These predicted values are then used to estimate poverty incidence and other poverty measures at a more granular level. The ADB project explored the use of luminosity and other satellite imagery data to complement the use of survey and census data for SAE.

[a] Asian Development Bank. 2017. Data for Development Project. https://www.adb.org/projects/51193-001/main.

A step-by-step approach for the use of big data in modeling for official statistics is presented in Box 3.8.

Box 3.8: Enhanced Step-by-Step Approach for the Use of Big Data in Official Statistics

The following steps outline a framework when making a decision with regard to when, how, and for what big data can be used in official statistics:

Step 1:   Specify the statistical problem (e.g., nowcasting).

Step 2:   Define an appropriate information technology environment for collecting, storing, treating, and analyzing big data.

Step 3:   Consider big data's potential usefulness within the statistical problems as defined in step 1.

Step 4:   Discuss issues related to the design of the exercise: possible big data sources, definition of the type of variables and/or information to be extracted from big data and other sources.

Step 5:   Assess big data accessibility and the quality of envisaged big data sources.

---

continued on next page

Box 3.8 *continued*

Step 6:   Explore big data-specific features and possible ways to move from unstructured to structured data.

Step 7:   Consider approaches to replace missing observations as well as to remove and correct outliers.

Step 8:   Consider ways to filter out seasonal and other very short-term components from big data.

Step 9:   Determine presence of bias in big data and the ways to correct it.

Step 10: Analyze the design of the econometric modeling strategy in case of the availability of numerical big data structured in time series form.

Step 11: Consider the statistical exploratory techniques to be used in case of nonnumerical or numerical but not structured big data.

Step 12: Evaluate the results mainly obtained in steps 10 and 11 (choice of benchmark model or nowcasts, evaluation metrics, criteria for assessing the significance of the accuracy and/or timeliness gains, the statistical and economic validity of the results, etc.)

Step 13: Consider the overall implementation of big data-based results within the regular production and dissemination process.

Source: D. Buono et al. 2018. *Enhanced step-by-step approach for the use of big data in modelling for official statistics.* Paper prepared for the 16th conference of the International Association for Official Statistics. 19–21 September. Paris.

Big Data Uses for Sustainable Development Goals Monitoring: Potential and (Current) Limitations

Findings from a 2017 survey of NSOs in Asia and the Pacific presented in an ADB brief provide insights from responding NSOs on factors affecting the use of big data to monitor the SDGs.[47] These include access to big data sources, technological infrastructure requirements, new skills acquisition, and concerns relating to *data privacy and security*.

On the other hand, a 2019 survey conducted by the UN Global Working Group on Big Data for Official Statistics showed that a large proportion of the 100 responding NSOs were already embracing big data but may require further information, guidance, development, and knowledge to remove barriers to working with big data (footnote 47). Table 3.2 summarizes the status of NSOs as compared with the factors and barriers in utilizing big data. The analysis presented in the Global Working Group on Big Data for Official Statistics report provide details on what are covered under the four key points (footnote 47).

[47]   ADB. 2019. Readiness of National Statistical Systems in Asia and the Pacific for Leveraging Big Data to Monitor the SDGs. *ADB Briefs*. No. 106. Manila. https://www.adb.org/sites/default/files/publication/491326/adb-brief-106-national-statistical-systems-big-data-sdgs.pdf. The ADB brief lists ongoing and/or completed big data-related initiatives in Asia and the Pacific as of 2017.

Table 3.2: Key Factors and Barriers in Utilizing Big Data for Official Statistics, Including Sustainable Development Goal Indicators

Key Points	Status	Barriers
1. Strategic coordination	Strategic coordination capacities are established. Many NSOs are engaged in big data projects. Ethics and quality frameworks are fairly established. Most NSOs view coordination with big data source owners inside their NSS as the lowest challenge.	Only one-third of all NSOs have overarching big data strategies in place and chief data officers only exist in some NSOs. The biggest challenge for NSOs is the collaboration with big data source owners outside the government.
2. Legal framework	Overall, respondents are aware of the fundamental role legal frameworks play in establishing big data projects. Many NSOs appear to have well-developed legal frameworks that penalize data disclosures and allow accredited access to their data.	Legal frameworks are still insufficient to regulate big data applications. Only a small share of NSOs rely on legal frameworks that guarantee access to big data.
3. IT infrastructure	The analysis shows a heterogeneous picture of the IT infrastructure. NSOs stated that basic IT infrastructure such as power supply and air-conditioning mostly met their needs, but they outlined struggles with storage facilities and computing power.	IT infrastructure is a central barrier to developing big data capacity; many NSOs need better on-site and off-site storage capacity. Only a few NSOs consider cloud storage a relevant option.
4. Human resources	NSOs recruit significantly more analysts than data scientists and prioritize up-skilling over hiring external staff to perform big data or data science techniques.	Most NSOs lack a competency framework to develop new skills to cope with big data (mobile phone, geospatial data) and new methodologies (machine learning).

IT = information technology, NSO = national statistics office, NSS = national statistical system.
Source: UN. 2020. *Background document for the Note by the Secretary-General transmitting the report of the Global Working Group on Big Data for Official Statistics* (E/CN.3/2020/24). Document prepared for the 51st session of the Statistical Commission. 3–6 March. New York. https://unstats.un.org/unsd/statcom/51st-session/documents/UN_BigData_report_v6.0-E.html.

Resources

Recommended Reading

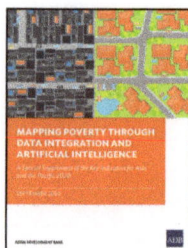

Asian Development Bank (ADB). 2020. *Mapping Poverty through Data Integration and Artificial Intelligence: A Special Supplement of the Key Indicators for Asia and the Pacific 2020*. Manila. https://www.adb.org/sites/default/files/publication/630406/mapping-poverty-ki2020-supplement.pdf.

This publication presents initial results of studies under the ADB knowledge initiative Data for Development, which aims to strengthen the capacity of national statistics offices (NSOs) in the Asia and Pacific region to meet the increasing data demands for effective policy making and for monitoring development goals and targets.

The approach demonstrates use of high-resolution satellite imagery, geospatial data, and powerful machine-learning algorithms to complement traditional data sources and conventional survey methods to estimate the magnitude of poverty. Statisticians from ADB's Statistics and Data Innovation Unit within the Economic Research and Regional Cooperation Department worked with the Philippine Statistics Authority, the National Statistical Office of Thailand, and the World Data Lab to examine the feasibility of poverty mapping using satellite imagery and associated geospatial data.

United Nations Statistics Division. 2016. *Report of the 2015 Big Data Survey*. Background document prepared for the 47th session of the Statistical Commission. 8–11 March. New York. https://unstats.un.org/bigdata/documents/reports/GWG%20Background%20document%20-%202016%20-6-Report-of-the-2015-Big-Data-Survey-E.pdf.
This report provides the outcome of a survey conducted from June to August 2015 among national statistics offices (NSOs) of 93 countries. The survey aimed to examine the situation regarding the steps undertaken by NSOs in relation to big data. It also examined the strategic visions of NSOs and their practical experience with big data. Participating countries reported the need for training and capacity building on big data topics (e.g., methodologies, estimation, and a quality framework) and conducting more pilot projects especially for developing countries. Further, NSOs relayed that easier access to big data can lower the threshold for undertaking a big data project.

3.6   Data Integration

Data integration is the process of combining or linking data from different sources to produce more comprehensive and disaggregated statistics and information. Most often, the data sources (e.g., censuses, surveys, administrative data, geospatial information) are designed and collected primarily without the intention of being used together. The benefits of bringing together information from different sources include the ability to answer a broader range of questions; examine underlying relationships between cross sections of society; and produce more timely, disaggregated statistics and at a greater frequency than traditional approaches alone. In addition, it is considered less time consuming and less costly when compared to other methods (such as surveys) and can also reduce respondent burden. However, NSOs also face challenges when integrating data, such as access to data, interoperability, technical capacity, and significant time and resource commitments.

There are many possible types of data integration. Five common types are (i) administrative sources integrated with survey and other traditional data, (ii) new data sources (such as big data) integrated with traditional data sources, (iii) geospatial data integrated with statistical information, (iv) micro-level data integrated with macro-level data, and (v) data from official sources validated with data from other sources. Box 3.9 provides examples of data integration outputs.

Box 3.9: Examples of Data Integration Outputs

(i)   An integrated dataset that serves as an input to produce official statistics

(ii)   A statistical model developed and produced using different sources to produce model-based information

(iii)   A dataset integrated for the purposes of micro-validation when some rules are defined to check the validity of the data in one dataset compared to another one

(iv)   Missing values imputed in a dataset using another dataset as the source for imputation

(v)   Datasets combined to produce a sampling frame for a survey

(vi)   Data from several subject-matter domains combined into one dataset that is the basis for the production of statistics (e.g., national accounts)

(vii)   Datasets from different subject-matter domains compared to check the quality and the validity of information produced (macro-validation)

(viii) Input from several sources integrated into one dataset to provide micro-data files for the researchers for scientific purposes

(ix)   Different sources used to apply proper statistical disclosure control methods on a micro-dataset

---

Example Case Studies

In an effort to build technical capacity, the UN Economic and Social Commission for Asia and the Pacific (ESCAP) supported two case studies on data integration. The first case study, from Bangladesh, focused on inequality and poverty indicators using nontraditional data sources (geospatial data) and a health survey.[48] The second case study, from Sri Lanka, focused on women's empowerment indicators using more traditional data sources (a labor force survey and a household and income and expenditure survey).[49]

Figure 3.3: Bangladesh and Sri Lanka Case Studies

Demographic Health Survey and Geo-covariate data integration: Case study on Bangladesh 2014

A Study on Combining Sample Surveys to Improve Data Availability on Selected SDG Indicators for Priority Policy Issues Identified for Economic Empowerment of Women in Sri Lanka

When it is difficult to obtain up-to-date geographic data through censuses and surveys, using publicly available geo-spatial data can lead to more timely, frequent and granular analyses in addition to increasing the availability of disaggregated statistics.

However, integrating data from geographic information systems with survey data requires extensive IT capability and analysis of the integrated data requires application of complicated statistical models.

Lack of common linking variables on sample surveys makes combining data sources complicated.

Inconsistency of the definitions, coverage, reference period and frequency of sample surveys adds to the complexity

Small sample size of some population groups hinders application of modeling for imputation of missing variables.

Given the cost and respondent burden of sample survey NSOs may consider switching to administrative data that can provide more timely and frequent data with more granularity.

Maintaining consistency of questions, response categories, and classifications across surveys facilitates data integration.

IT = information technology, NSO = national statistics office, SDG = Sustainable Development Goal.

Sources: Adapted from A. Yazdani. 2019. Using Data Integration to Meet the Ambitions of the 2030 Agenda. *United Nations Economic and Social Commission for Asia and the Pacific blog.* 3 July. https://www.unescap.org/blog/using-data-integration-meet-ambitions-2030-agenda; Y. Wang. 2019. *Report: DHS and Geo-covariates data integration—Case study on Bangladesh survey 2014.* Available from https://communities.unescap.org/system/files/report_dhs_and_geo-covariates_data_integration_bangladesh_survey_2014.pdf.; and G. De Silva et al. 2019. *Improving data availability for economic empowerment of women in Sri Lanka: A study on data integration for monitoring the SDGs.* Paper prepared for Asia-Pacific Economic Statistics Week 2019. 17–19 June. Bangkok. https://communities.unescap.org/system/files/improving_data_availability_for_economic_empowerment_of_women_in_sri_lanka.pdf.

---

[48]   Y. Wang. 2019. *Report: DHS and Geo-covariates data integration—Case study on Bangladesh survey 2014.* https://communities.unescap.org/system/files/report_dhs_and_geo-covariates_data_integration_bangladesh_survey_2014.pdf.

[49]   G. De Silva et al. 2019. *Improving data availability for economic empowerment of women in Sri Lanka: A study on data integration for monitoring the SDGs.* Paper prepared for Asia-Pacific Economic Statistics Week 2019. 17–19 June. Bangkok. https://www.unescap.org/sites/default/files/2.1%20ESCAP_Gamini%20SL.pdf.

Resources providing guidance on applications of data integration for generating data for specific vulnerable populations are briefly described in Box 3.10.

Box 3.10: Methods for Data Integration with Specific Applications

a. Persons with Disabilities

The Model Disability Survey (MDS), developed by the World Health Organization and the World Bank, is a general population household survey that provides detailed and nuanced information about how people with and without disabilities conduct their lives and the difficulties they encounter, regardless of any underlying health condition or impairment.[a] The brief version of the MDS can also be integrated in other surveys. For example, it was implemented as a module with the Gallup World Poll in India, the Lao People's Democratic Republic, and Tajikistan. The Gallup World Poll is the only global study of its kind and contains dozens of questions on a variety of environmental factors relevant to the disability experience, like economic empowerment, access to clean water, access to nutritious food, citizen engagement, and public safety. The integration of the brief MDS with the Gallup World Poll was implemented in these three countries as a means of testing a new efficient way of obtaining high-quality, standardized, and comprehensive disability data globally. The combination of the brief MDS with the World Poll variables not only allows for the disaggregation of key World Poll indicators by level of disability, but it also allows users to go beyond disaggregation and analyze the complex ways in which all of these societal factors influence disability, and vice versa.[b]

The Washington Group on Disability Statistics also provides additional data collection tools for compiling disability statistics.[c]

b. Migration

The United Nations Economic Commission for Europe (UNECE) produced Guidance on Data Integration for Measuring Migration, which included case studies on data integration in various national contexts and best practice principles for national statistics offices (NSOs).[d]

c. Refugees or Internally Displaced Persons

The Expert Group on Refugee and Internally Displaced Persons Statistics provides general recommendations on data integration, while the expert group's Compilers' Manual presents the main steps related to data integration and an overview on the possible data integration techniques that can help and guide practitioners in NSOs interested in applying data integration to refugee and internally displaced persons statistics.[d]

d. Urban and/or Slum Areas

The United Nations Human Settlements Programme uses the Demographic Health Surveys, Multiple Indicator Cluster Surveys, and Living Standards Measurement Study modules for household characteristics with regard to measurement of some Sustainable Development Goal indicators.[e]

---

[a] World Health Organization. MDS. https://www.who.int/disabilities/data/mds/en/.

[b] United Nations. E/CN.3/2020/34. *Disability Statistics*. Joint report of the Secretary-General, the Washington Group on Disability Statistics and international agencies. https://unstats.un.org/unsd/statcom/51st-session/documents/2020-34-DisabilityStats-Rev-EE.pdf.

[c] For the 49th Session of the United Nations Statistical Commission, the Washington Group on Disability Statistics prepared a background document which lists some recommendations for disaggregation. https://unstats.un.org/unsd/statcom/49th-session/documents/BG-Item3n-WG-on-Disability-Statistics-E.pdf. Additional details are also provided through the group's webpage: https://www.washingtongroup-disability.com/resources/disaggregation-and-sdgs/.

[d] UNECE. 2019. *Guidance on Data Integration for Measuring Migration*. Geneva. http://www.unece.org/fileadmin/DAM/stats/publications/2018/ECECESSTAT20186.pdf.

[e] UNHCR. *Refugee Data Finder*. Methodology. https://www.unhcr.org/refugee-statistics/methodology/; Expert Group on Refugee and Internally Displaced Persons Statistics. 2018. *International Recommendations on Refugee Statistics*. https://unstats.un.org/unsd/demographic-social/Standards-and-Methods/files/Principles_and_Recommendations/International-Migration/2018_1746_EN_08-E.pdf; Expert Group on Refugee and Internally Displaced Persons Statistics. 2020. *Compilers' Manual on Displacement Statistics*. Background document prepared for the 51st session of the Statistical Commission. 3–6 March. New York. https://unstats.un.org/unsd/statcom/51st-session/documents/BG-item-3n-compilers-manual-E.pdf; and United Nations Human Settlements Programme. 2019. *The Urban SDG Monitoring Series*. Issue 1. February 2019. 2019. http://unhabitat.org.ir/wp-content/uploads/2019/03/SDG-11.1.1-Newsletter_2.1.pdf (accessed 9 March 2021).

General Guidance on Data Integration Methods

Several guidance documents and reviews of data integration have been developed by NSOs and other regional organizations.

(i)   Statistics New Zealand's *Data integration manual: 2nd edition* includes best practices and insights gained from its experience in integrating data. The document outlines basic concepts, theories, and processes involved in data integration along with practical advice and operational aspects, including privacy concerns.[50]

(ii)   The United Nations Economic Commission for Europe (UNECE) and the Conference of European Statisticians conducted an in-depth review of data integration aimed to address a general lack of guidance and overview of experiences. The document outlines types of data integration, a general framework, and a broad approach as well as opportunities, challenges, skills, and resources needed.[51] It includes several types of data integration, such as survey and administrative sources, survey and new data sources (including big data), traditional sources with geospatial information, and integrating data for validating official statistics.

(iii) UNECE's *A Guide to Data Integration for Official Statistics (version 2.0)* provides practical advice and information to advance data integration activities by statistical organizations, and information about issues that statistical organizations have or should consider in their work on data integration.[52]

(iv)   UN ESCAP's Stat Brief titled "Integrated Statistics: A journey worthwhile" focuses on a quick reference document on process integration and data integration, addressing delivery issues relevant to each, while also outlining different sources common for official statistics production.[53]

(v)   FAO details techniques and guidelines for using remote sensing and other agricultural censuses and surveys for agricultural statistics including in the *Handbook on Remote Sensing for Agricultural Statistics,* the *Technical Report on Reconciling Data from Agricultural Censuses and Surveys,* and additional publications on remote sensing and geographic information and data integration using small area estimation.[54]

---

[50] Statistics New Zealand. 2015. *Data and Statistics integration manual: 2nd edition.* Wellington. https://ndhadeliver.natlib.govt.nz/delivery/DeliveryManagerServlet?dps_pid=IE25102655; New Zealand. Integrated data. https://www.stats.govt.nz/integrated-data/.

[51] UNECE and the Conference of European Statisticians. 2017. *In-depth review of data integration.* Note prepared for the meeting of the Conference of European Statisticians 2016/2017 Bureau. 14–15 February. Geneva. http://www.unece.org/fileadmin/DAM/stats/documents/ece/ces/bur/2017/February/02_in-depth_review_data_integration_final.pdf; and UNECE. *Data integration.* https://www.unece.org/stats/ces/in-depth-reviews/geospatial2.html.

[52] United Nations Economic Commission for Europe (UNECE). 2018. *A Guide to Data Integration for Official Statistics.* https://statswiki.unece.org/spaces/flyingpdf/pdfpageexport.action?pageId=129171769.

[53] UN ESCAP. 2019. *Integrated Statistics: A journey worthwhile.* Stats Brief. Issue no. 19. https://www.unescap.org/sites/default/files/Stats_Brief_Issue19_Jul2019_Integrated_Statistics.pdf.

[54] http://gsars.org/en/tag/geoinfo/.

(vi)   *The Global Statistical Geospatial Framework* developed by the UN Global Geospatial Information Management Secretariat, facilitates the integration of statistical and geospatial information through the application of five principles and supporting key elements.[55] These data can also be integrated with statistical, geospatial, and other information to inform and facilitate data-driven and evidence-based decision-making, in particular for the 2030 Agenda for Sustainable Development and the SDGs.

(vii) *The Territorial Dimension in SDG Indicators: Geospatial Data Analysis and its Integration with Statistical Data* report from the UN Global Geospatial Information Management for Europe addresses the territorial dimension of the SDGs and the contribution of geospatial information integrated with statistical data for disaggregated, aggregated, mapped, and visualized information.[56]

---

[55]   UN Global Geospatial Information Management Secretariat. 2019. *The Global Statistical Geospatial Framework.* New York. http://ggim.un.org/meetings/GGIM-committee/9th-Session/documents/The_GSGF.pdf.

[56]   United Nations Committee of Experts on Global Geospatial Information Management for Europe. 2019. *The territorial dimension in SDG indicators: geospatial data analysis and its integration with statistical data.* Lisbon. https://un-ggim-europe.org/wp-content/uploads/2019/05/UN_GGIM_08_05_2019-The-territorial-dimension-in-SDG-indicators-Final.pdf.

CHAPTER 4

ANALYSIS OF DISAGGREGATED DATA IN AID OF LEAVE NO ONE BEHIND

Overview

Disaggregated data are important for informing policies and designing programs for vulnerable groups of the population, who can be further left behind in the development agenda. However, there are several points to consider in analyzing disaggregated data before these data can be translated into policy inputs, including availability of micro-data, allocation of time and resources, and data reliability.

This chapter provides an overview of *multilevel disaggregation analysis* of Sustainable Development Goal (SDG) indicators and illustrates the application of this analysis through specific case studies on poverty and gender and intersectionality, and through the introduction of existing software on equity assessments. The chapter also demonstrates the importance of data visualization in telling stories beyond the inequality numbers.

4.1 Basics

Examining Equity Issues with Disaggregated Data

As discussed in the Introduction and Chapters 1 and 2, the 2030 Agenda for Sustainable Development highlights the importance of leaving no one behind. Several goals—including no poverty (SDG 1), zero hunger (SDG 2), gender equality (SDG 5), and reduced inequalities (SDG 10)—directly aim to tackle inequality, while other goals—including good health and well-being (SDG 3), quality education (SDG 4), clean water and sanitation (SDG 6), affordable and clean energy (SDG 7), and decent work and economic growth (SDG 8)—place emphasis on universality and inclusion, which build a strong agenda for examining equity issues.

Data help in discerning emerging policy concerns, informing policy choices and the design of public interventions, and monitoring policy implementation as well as evaluating impact. Disaggregated data helps to describe the conditions and needs of vulnerable groups in a society, e.g., youth, elderly, people with disabilities, indigenous people, people living with HIV/AIDS, refugees, and ethnic minorities. Without disaggregated data, we do not know if policies and interventions are leaving the most vulnerable people even further behind. The availability of disaggregated data is imperative for examining inequities. Disaggregated data can assist in evaluating how specific demographic groups are performing in achieving outcomes (e.g., education, labor, health). They can also help in considering whether policies are narrowing gaps, and in revealing patterns that can be masked by aggregate data. Disaggregated data can facilitate identifying needs so that resources can be allocated more equitably. Further, disaggregated data can also improve the monitoring of equity in resources and outcomes.

Analysis Objectives and Plan

The availability of micro-data provides flexibility to generate data and summary measures at different aggregation or disaggregation levels. If micro-data are formatted consistently, specialized tools can be designed to automate the production of summary measures and serve routine purposes. For instance, consider country diagnostics of poverty, which require estimates of poverty incidence (and profiles of the poor) sourced from household surveys that collect information on monetary indicators on living conditions (such as income and/or expenditure) and other welfare indicators.[57] Often, such poverty analysis involves a considerable amount of time and resources to produce a set of template tables and graphs that describe poverty and inequality.

Drawing disaggregated information from micro-data requires examination of data reliability. In some cases, micro-data do not provide adequate information for every desired level of disaggregation. In surveys, for instance, the sample size for a desired disaggregation level may be too small to provide reliable estimates, which demonstrates the limitations of estimates. In other cases, data producers and compilers do not publish disaggregated data when its reliability does not meet a predetermined threshold.

Box 4.1: Example of the Analysis Tool—Automated Development Economics Poverty Tables (ADePT)

The World Bank designed the Automated Development Economics Poverty Tables (ADePT) software to simplify and speed up its analytical work on obtaining poverty profiles, making use of either individual- or household-level micro-data.[a] This approach helps minimize errors in poverty profiling, while introducing techniques and methods of applied economic analysis to a wide audience of poverty stakeholders. The ADePT software, available for free, generates a standard set of tables and graphs on poverty and inequality, data disaggregation on poverty statistics (for standard demographic groups), as well as regressions on monetary indicators of poverty (thus identifying determinants of poverty). In addition to poverty and inequality, ADePT has modules on labor, gender, social protection, education, health, food security, and agriculture. By automating the production of template tables that are commonly used for development research, the availability of a software platform such as ADePT gives more time for researchers to carefully examine disaggregated data and the messages it conveys.

[a] World Bank. ADePT. https://www.worldbank.org/en/topic/health/brief/adept-resource-center.

4.2   Examining Multilevel Disaggregation

To identify those furthest behind, assessment is conducted that features the simultaneous analysis of disaggregated data on several variables that define the relevant disaggregation dimensions, i.e., multilevel disaggregation. In this guidebook, this type of analysis is referred to as *"multilevel disaggregation analysis"* or *"multilevel analysis."*

---

[57]   J. Haughton and S. Khandker. 2009. *Handbook on Poverty and Inequality.* Washington, DC: The World Bank. http://documents1. worldbank.org/curated/en/488081468157174849/pdf/483380PUB0Pove101OFFICIAL0USE0ONLY1.pdf.

Example: Poverty Rates, Philippines

As countries consolidate their efforts to realize the SDGs related to poverty reduction, it is the responsibility of every sector to ask how they can contribute to building equity in living standards and ensure that the poorest of the poor are not left behind. While a great amount of data is collected about poverty, only a fraction provides the detail that is needed by policy makers to design and assess the impact of a well-targeted intervention program on different equity dimensions. With the availability of granular data, socioeconomic planners can capture and use the necessary evidence to understand and respond to inequity in poverty outcomes.

The availability of subnational poverty rate estimates has increased since 2000, typically for large geographical administrative areas as illustrated in Figure 4.1 for the 17 *regions* of the Philippines.[58]

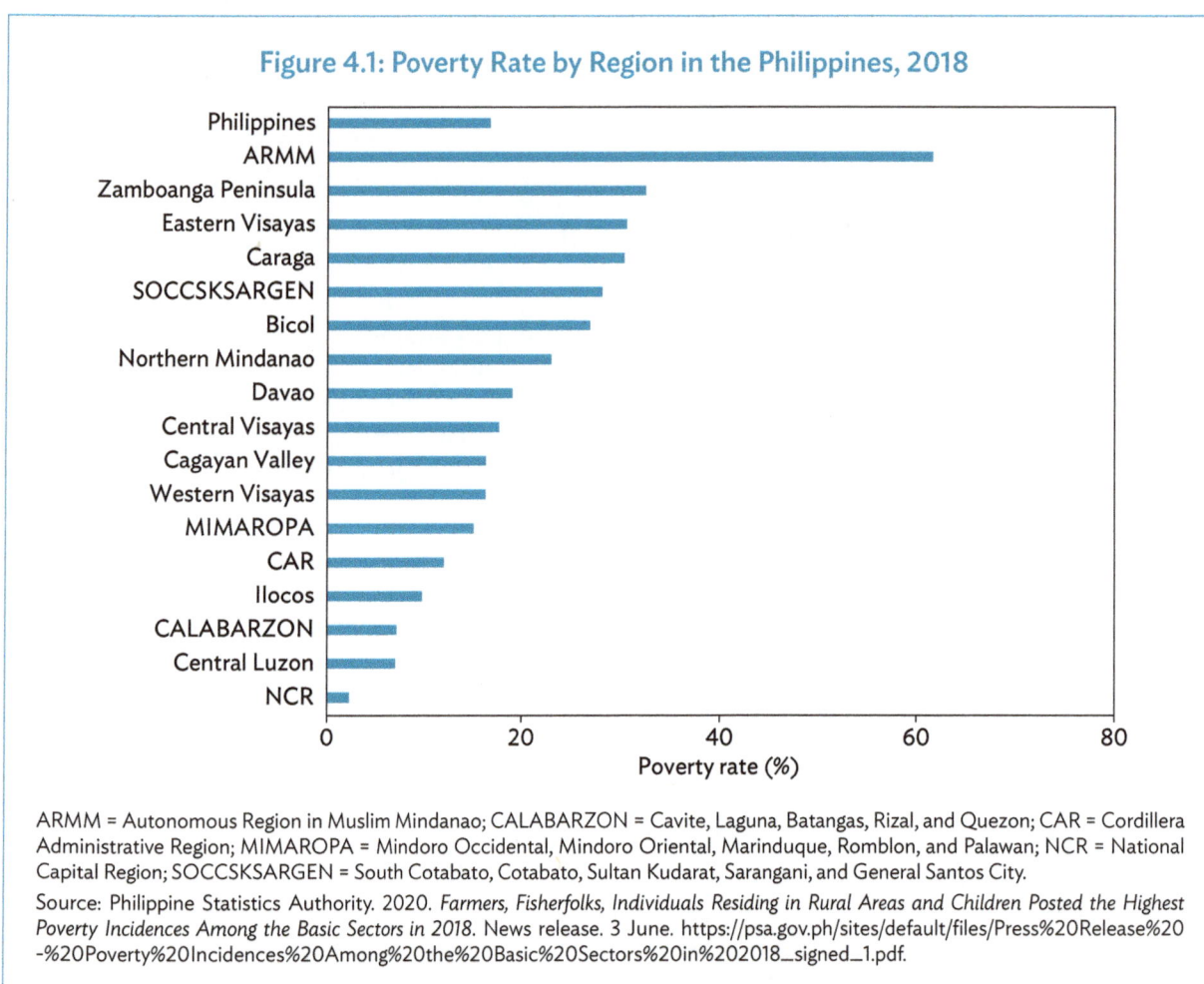

Figure 4.1: Poverty Rate by Region in the Philippines, 2018

ARMM = Autonomous Region in Muslim Mindanao; CALABARZON = Cavite, Laguna, Batangas, Rizal, and Quezon; CAR = Cordillera Administrative Region; MIMAROPA = Mindoro Occidental, Mindoro Oriental, Marinduque, Romblon, and Palawan; NCR = National Capital Region; SOCCSKSARGEN = South Cotabato, Cotabato, Sultan Kudarat, Sarangani, and General Santos City.

Source: Philippine Statistics Authority. 2020. *Farmers, Fisherfolks, Individuals Residing in Rural Areas and Children Posted the Highest Poverty Incidences Among the Basic Sectors in 2018.* News release. 3 June. https://psa.gov.ph/sites/default/files/Press%20Release%20-%20Poverty%20Incidences%20Among%20the%20Basic%20Sectors%20in%202018_signed_1.pdf.

---

[58]   Regions are the highest levels of geographic disaggregation in the Philippines. Regions are further subdivided into provinces, and provinces into municipalities and cities.

Even at this high level of disaggregation, it is clear that much remains to be done in terms of promoting further geographic equity in poverty reduction, as significant pockets of poverty still remain in many areas of the southern Philippines like the Autonomous Region in Muslim Mindanao and Zamboanga Peninsula.

Until 2000, reliable data on poverty in specific municipalities of the Philippines were sparse because the Family Income and Expenditure Survey, which is used to compile official poverty statistics in the country, was designed to provide reliable estimates at higher geographic levels. With the efforts of government statisticians and international development partners, the country started compiling the 2000 municipal- and city-level data on poverty in 2005. Based on the 2003 municipal- and city-level data on poverty, Siayan municipality in the Zamboanga Peninsula was identified as one of the poorest municipalities in the Philippines, with the proportion of the population living below the national poverty line estimated to reach as high as 97.5%.[59]

These disaggregated statistics shed light on the prevalence of poverty in Siayan, where the majority of the population is at risk of socioeconomic vulnerabilities and exclusion. Since these poverty estimates became available in 2009, the country's socioeconomic planners, policy makers, and development institutions worked to turn this situation around and improve the lives of Siayan's population. In fact, poverty estimates compiled by the Philippine Statistics Authority showed that the proportion of the municipality's population living below the poverty line dropped to 68.4% in 2015. For the 2012 and 2015 estimation periods, Siayan has graduated from the list of 10 poorest municipalities in the country.

In addition to geographically disaggregated poverty data, the Philippine Statistics Authority continues to disaggregate poverty statistics by different dimensions to provide empirical evidence for monitoring poverty and assessing the impact of programs designed to arrest socioeconomic decline. For instance, to provide inputs for the implementation of the country's *Social Reform and Poverty Alleviation Act of 1998*, which promotes an area-based, sector, and focused intervention to poverty alleviation, the Philippine Statistics Authority has been producing poverty statistics disaggregated by basic sector. The latest statistics show (Figure 4.2) that the prevalence of poverty among farmers, fisherfolk, people living in rural areas, and children is higher than the national average.[60] These results highlight the need for better poverty alleviation programs targeted to these population groups.

---

[59]   Philippine Statistics Authority. 2009. *2003 City and Municipal Level Poverty Estimates.* https://psa.gov.ph/sites/default/files/2003%20SAE%20of%20poverty%20%28Full%20Report%29_0.pdf.

[60]   Philippine Statistics Authority. 2020. *Farmers, Fisherfolks, Individuals Residing in Rural Areas and Children Posted the Highest Poverty Incidences Among the Basic Sectors in 2018.* News release. 3 June. https://psa.gov.ph/sites/default/files/Press%20Release%20-%20Poverty%20Incidences%20Among%20the%20Basic%20Sectors%20in%202018_signed_1.pdf.

Figure 4.2: Poverty Rate by Basic Sector in the Philippines, 2018

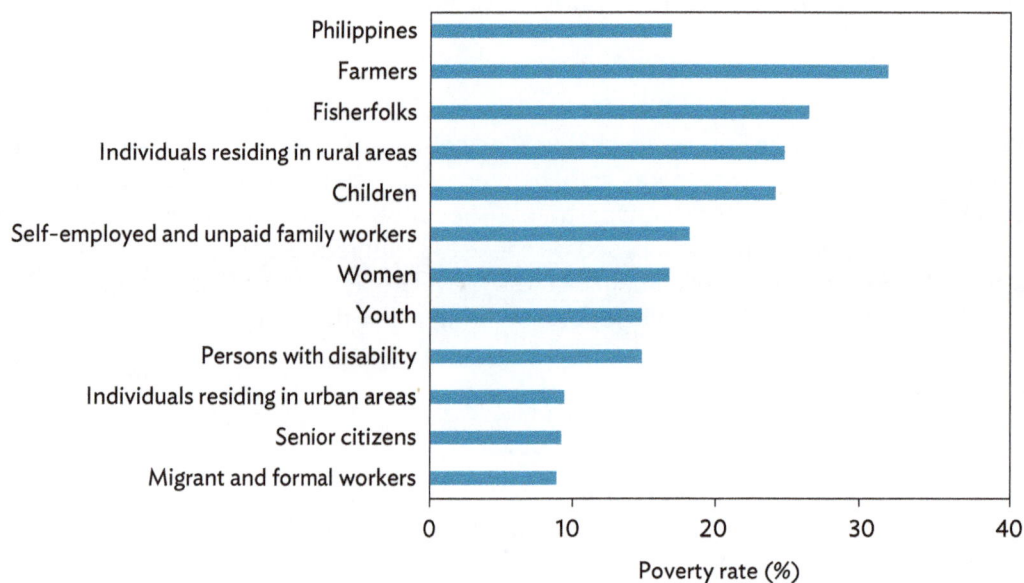

Source: Philippine Statistics Authority. 2020. *Farmers, Fisherfolks, Individuals Residing in Rural Areas and Children Posted the Highest Poverty Incidences Among the Basic Sectors in 2018.* News release. 3 June. https://psa.gov.ph/sites/default/files/Press%20Release%20-%20Poverty%20Incidences%20Among%20the%20Basic%20Sectors%20in%202018_signed_1.pdf.

In summary, the availability of disaggregated data on poverty facilitates a more layered and nuanced analysis on equity issues in poverty reduction efforts.

Example: Gender and Intersectionality

The United Nations (UN) General Assembly adopted by consensus Resolution 70/1: Transforming our world: the 2030 Agenda for Sustainable Development. The resolution states the following: "Realizing gender equality and the empowerment of women and girls will make a crucial contribution to progress across all the Goals and targets."[61] The prioritization of gender equality and women's rights is reflected in a crosscutting manner throughout the 2030 Agenda, including the declaration, goals, targets and indicators, means of implementation, and follow-up and review.

---

[61]   UN General Assembly. 2015. *Resolution adopted by the General Assembly on 25 September 2015: Transforming our world—the 2030 Agenda for Sustainable Development (70/1).* New York. p. 6. https://www.un.org/en/development/desa/population/migration/generalassembly/docs/globalcompact/A_RES_70_1_E.pdf.

Box 4.2: Measurement of Gender and Intersecting Inequalities

Inequalities are usually interconnected in ways that worsen poverty. Thus, the specific needs of the most disadvantaged segments of the population should be recognized and assessed so they can inform political dialogues and effect the necessary change.

When evidence used to formulate policies fall short of highlighting inequalities, the results tend to leave the most vulnerable people behind. Further, inadequate data are likely to result to inadequate responses.

Measuring intersecting inequalities entails generating more granular data by sex, age, and other sociodemographic characteristics (e.g., class, race, location, disability, educational level, migratory status, etc.). It also requires cautious critical thinking, selecting subjects and asking questions about how various segments of population may be affected. Deliberating and selecting subjects, which must include participation from marginalized segments of the population, is specifically critical but are regularly missing, making data less relevant.[a]

The "Counted and Visible: Global Conference on the measurement of gender and intersecting inequalities" conference, organized on 26 February 2020 by the United Nations (UN) Entity for Gender Equality and the Empowerment of Women (UN Women) in collaboration with the UN Statistics Division, tackled challenges and demonstrated initiatives on how to measure intersecting inequalities from a gender perspective.[b] The various speakers, drawn from government statisticians, policy makers, civil society practitioners, and development organizations, shared information on (i) what gender, intersectionality, and leave no one behind (LNOB) means for realizing the Sustainable Development Goals; (ii) how gender, intersectionality, and LNOB are translated into data production and analysis; (iii) how (a) vulnerable groups traditionally rendered invisible in social statistics and (b) examples of how data on gender and intersecting inequalities can be strategically used to inform policies and advocacy on gender equality.

[a] P. Seck. 2020. Integrate intersecting inequalities to leave no one behind. United Nations World Data Forum Blog. 13 October. https://unstats.un.org/unsd/undataforum/blog/Integrate-intersecting-inequalities-to-leave-no-one-behind/.

[b] UN Women. Counted and Visible: Global Conference on the measurement of gender and intersecting inequalities. https://data.unwomen.org/news/counted-and-visible-global-conference-measurement-gender-and-intersecting-inequalities.

Women and girls are often at risk of experiencing disadvantage. Besides sex-based discrimination, they may experience other overlapping forms of discrimination associated with socioeconomic characteristics, such as living in rural areas or poor households. These groups of women facing multiple forms of discrimination will experience severe forms of deprivation.[62]

---

[62] UN Entity for Gender Equality and the Empowerment of Women (UN Women). 2018. *Turning Promises into Action: Gender Equality in the 2030 Agenda for Sustainable Development.* New York. https://www.unwomen.org/-/media/headquarters/ attachments/sections/library/publications/2018/sdg-report-gender-equality-in-the-2030-agenda-for-sustainable-development-2018-en.pdf?la=en&vs=4332.

The analysis that would be most impactful would involve looking at multiple, contextually relevant socioeconomic characteristics that can be potential causes or drivers of inequality. The rationale is that an individual can be at the intersection of multiple identities that push them downward on the ladder of progress. For instance, Figure 4.3, which summarizes country data on illiteracy rates among those aged 15 to 49 by sex and economic status during 2005–2015, shows gaps not only between the poor and the rich, but also between women and men across countries, mostly to the disadvantage of women among the poorest wealth quintile.

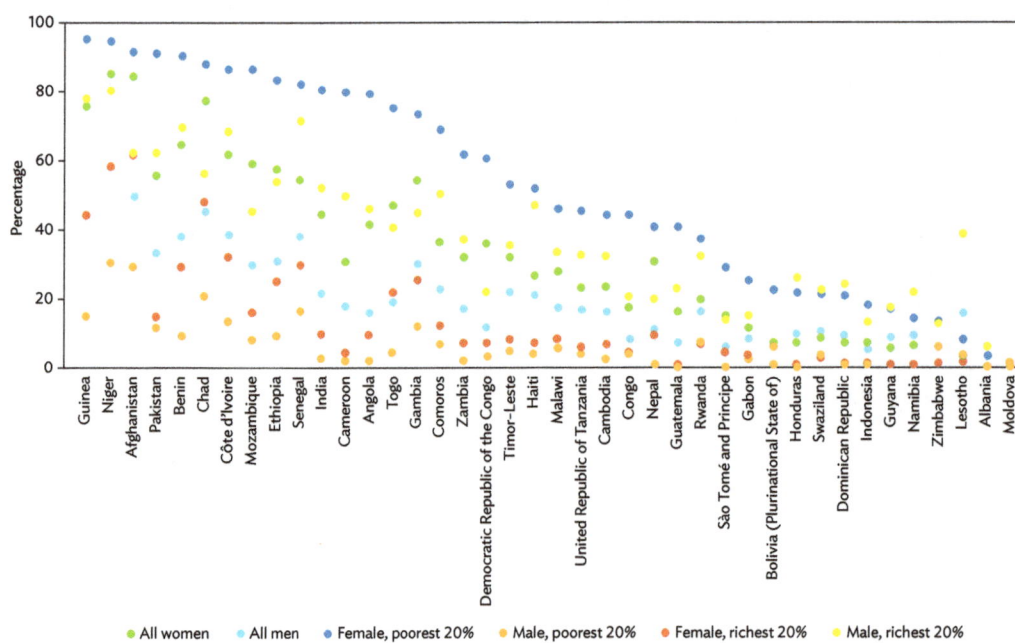

Figure 4.3: Illiteracy Rate among Population Aged 15–49, by Sex and Wealth Quintiles, 2005–2016

Source: Adapted from United Nations Entity for Gender Equality and the Empowerment of Women (UN Women). 2018. *Turning Promises into Action: Gender Equality in the 2030 Agenda for Sustainable Development*. New York. Available from https://www.unwomen.org/-/media/headquarters/attachments/sections/library/publications/2018/sdg-report-gender-equality-in-the-2030-agenda-for-sustainable-development-2018-en.pdf?la=en&vs=4332.

Figure 4.4 shows that while 40.2% of women aged 18–49 in Pakistan were married or in a union before 18 years old (2012-2013), disaggregated data reveals that the gap in corresponding percentages between the poorest in the rural areas (58.5%) and the richest in urban areas (23.9%) is as much as 34.6 percentage points.

Figure 4.4: Proportion of Women Aged 18–49 Who Were Married or in a Union before Age 18 in Pakistan, 2012-2013

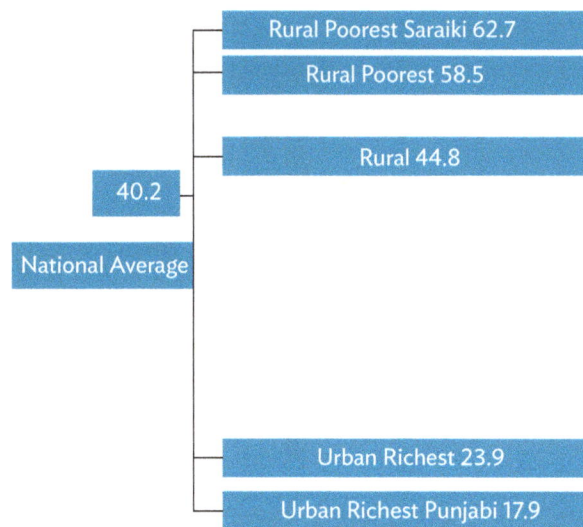

Rural Poorest Saraiki 62.7

Rural Poorest 58.5

Rural 44.8

40.2

National Average

Urban Richest 23.9

Urban Richest Punjabi 17.9

Source: Adapted from United Nations Entity for Gender Equality and the Empowerment of Women (UN Women). 2019. *Gender data and multi-level disaggregation: an LNOB perspective to SDG monitoring.* Presentation prepared for the International Workshop on Data Disaggregation for Sustainable Development Goals. 29 January. Bangkok. Available from https://unstats. un.org/sdgs/files/meetings/sdg-inter-workshop-jan-2019/Session%208.a_UNWomen_Gender%20data%20and%20 multi%20level%20disaggregation.pdf.

Similar patterns of national aggregates masking differences among demographic groups in Nigeria are illustrated in Figure 4.5. While 46.8% of women in Nigeria aged 18–49 were married or in a union before 18, the proportions are much larger (80%–90% of women) among the poorest in the rural population from the Fulani and Hausa ethnic groups, as compared to about 10% of the Yoruba females among the richest quintile residing in urban areas.

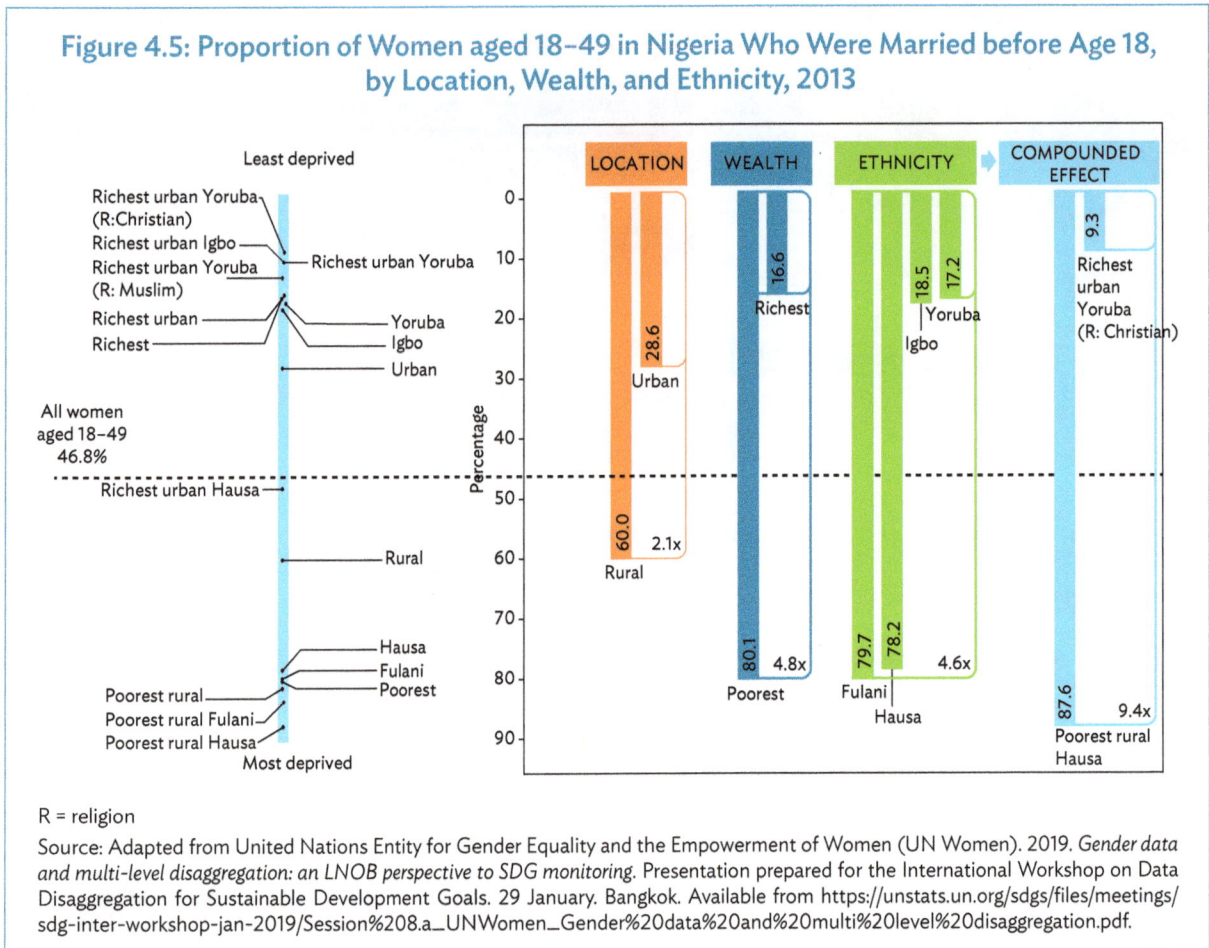

Figure 4.5: Proportion of Women aged 18–49 in Nigeria Who Were Married before Age 18, by Location, Wealth, and Ethnicity, 2013

R = religion

Source: Adapted from United Nations Entity for Gender Equality and the Empowerment of Women (UN Women). 2019. *Gender data and multi-level disaggregation: an LNOB perspective to SDG monitoring*. Presentation prepared for the International Workshop on Data Disaggregation for Sustainable Development Goals. 29 January. Bangkok. Available from https://unstats.un.org/sdgs/files/meetings/sdg-inter-workshop-jan-2019/Session%208.a_UNWomen_Gender%20data%20and%20multi%20level%20disaggregation.pdf.

The analyses provided in Figures 4.3–4.5 can be carried out using a framework for LNOB analysis developed by the UN Entity for Gender Equality and the Empowerment of Women (UN Women). A schematic diagram of the framework is shown in Figure 4.6.

Figure 4.6: Framework for Leave No One Behind Analysis

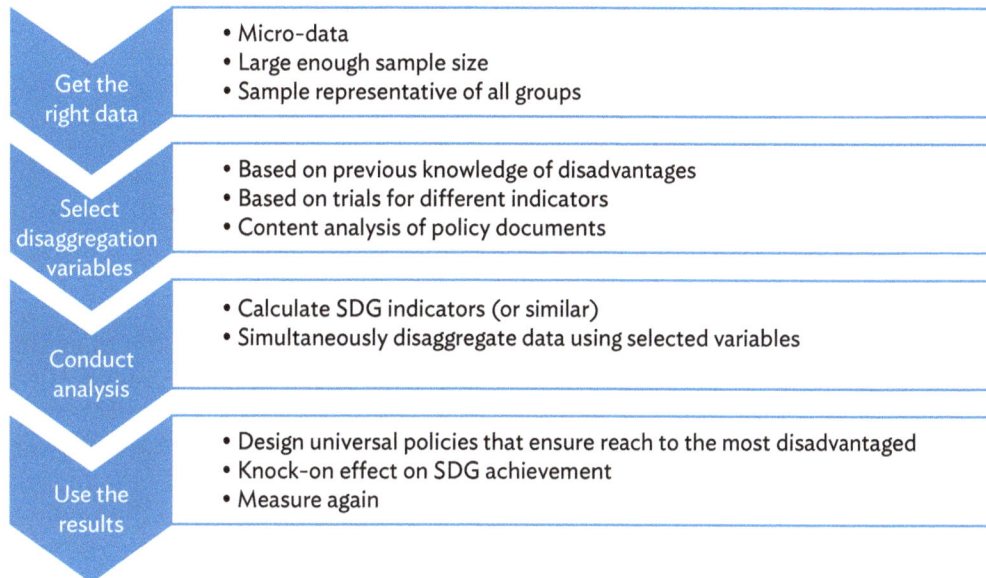

Get the right data
- Micro-data
- Large enough sample size
- Sample representative of all groups

Select disaggregation variables
- Based on previous knowledge of disadvantages
- Based on trials for different indicators
- Content analysis of policy documents

Conduct analysis
- Calculate SDG indicators (or similar)
- Simultaneously disaggregate data using selected variables

Use the results
- Design universal policies that ensure reach to the most disadvantaged
- Knock-on effect on SDG achievement
- Measure again

SDG = Sustainable Development Goal.

Source: Adapted from United Nations Entity for Gender Equality and the Empowerment of Women (UN Women). 2020. *Module 7: Multilevel Disaggregation Analysis to Monitor the SDGs from a Leave No One Behind Perspective—Training Syllabus.* Available from https://data.unwomen.org/sites/default/files/documents/Asia-Pacific-Training-Curriculum/Module7/Module7_Syllabus_LNOB.pdf.

Recommended Reading

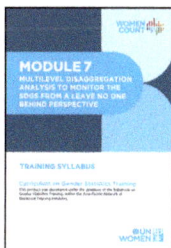

United Nations Entity for Gender Equality and the Empowerment of Women (UN Women). 2020. *Module 7: Multilevel Disaggregation Analysis to Monitor the SDGs from a Leave No One Behind Perspective—Training Syllabus.* https://data.unwomen.org/sites/default/files/documents/Asia-Pacific-Training-Curriculum/Module7/Module7_Syllabus_LNOB.pdf.

This training module provides the framework for leave no one behind analysis to carry out multilevel disaggregation analysis on gender and intersectionalities.

4.3   Equity Assessments and Disparity Analysis: Health Equity Assessment Toolkit

To support countries in measuring and monitoring health inequalities, the World Health Organization (WHO) developed the Health Equity Assessment Toolkit (HEAT), a software application that facilitates the assessment of within-country health inequalities.[63] Inequalities can be assessed using disaggregated data and summary measures that are visualized in a variety of interactive graphs, maps, and tables. HEAT is available in two editions:

(i)   HEAT, the built-in database edition, which contains the WHO Health Equity Monitor database; and

(ii)   HEAT Plus, the upload database edition, which allows users to upload their own datasets and analyze inequalities using their data.

HEAT, the built-in database edition of the toolkit, uses disaggregated data from the WHO Health Equity Monitor database, which in the 2019 update contained more than 30 reproductive, maternal, newborn, and child health indicators, disaggregated by six dimensions of inequality: economic status, education, place of residence, subnational region, age, and sex (where applicable).[64] The disaggregated data are based on a reanalysis of more than 360 Demographic and Health Surveys (DHS), Multiple Indicator Cluster Surveys (MICS), and Reproductive Health Surveys conducted in 112 countries from 1991 to 2017.[65] More than 100 (95%) countries are low- or middle-income, and for 88 countries (79%), data are available for at least two time points.

---

[63]   WHO. HEAT. https://www.who.int/gho/health_equity/assessment_toolkit/en/.

[64]   WHO. Health Equity Monitor Database. https://www.who.int/data/gho/health-equity/health-equity-monitor-database.

[65]   For information on the DHS, refer to the website https://dhsprogram.com/. For information on the MICS, refer to the website https://mics.unicef.org/. For information on Reproductive Health Surveys refer to the website https://www.cdc.gov/reproductivehealth/global/tools/surveys.htm.

The bar graphs in Figure 4.7 are taken from the online version of HEAT, pertaining to under-5 mortality rates in Bangladesh, disaggregated by sex.[66]

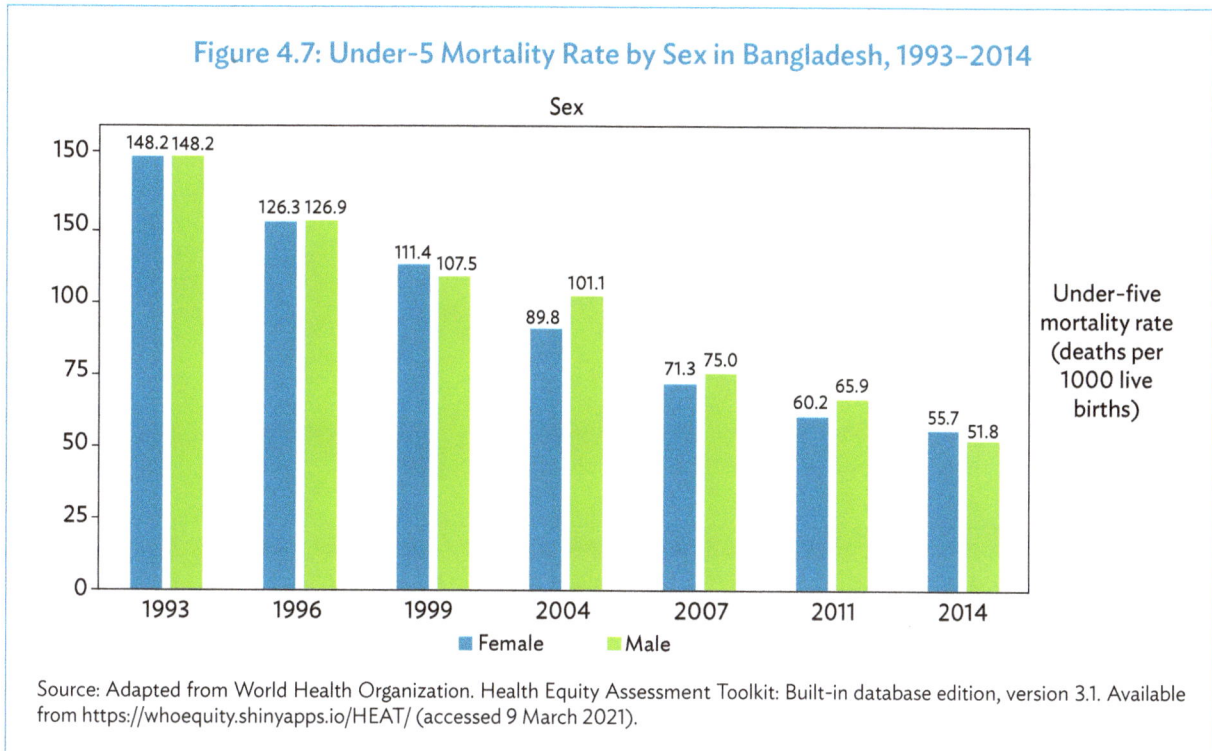

Figure 4.7: Under-5 Mortality Rate by Sex in Bangladesh, 1993–2014

Sex

Year	Female	Male
1993	148.2	148.2
1996	126.3	126.9
1999	111.4	107.5
2004	89.8	101.1
2007	71.3	75.0
2011	60.2	65.9
2014	55.7	51.8

Under-five mortality rate (deaths per 1000 live births)

■ Female ■ Male

Source: Adapted from World Health Organization. Health Equity Assessment Toolkit: Built-in database edition, version 3.1. Available from https://whoequity.shinyapps.io/HEAT/ (accessed 9 March 2021).

Figure 4.8 shows how child deaths in Bangladesh dropped significantly during 1993–2014. Further, it shows that gaps in child deaths between the different wealth quintiles have narrowed considerably over the same time period. In particular, the difference in the number of deaths among children below 5 between the richest and the poorest quintiles decreased from 87.3 deaths per 1,000 live births in 1993 to 24.5 deaths per 1,000 live births in 2014. The ratio of under-5 mortality rate in the poorest to richest quintile ranged from 2.0 in 2011 to 1.7 in 2014.

---

[66]   WHO. HEAT: Built-in database edition, version 3.1. https://whoequity.shinyapps.io/HEAT/.

Figure 4.8: Under-5 Mortality Rate by Economic Status in Bangladesh, 1993–2014

Bangladesh (DHS, 1993, 1996, 1999, 2004, 2007, 2011, 2014)
Economic status

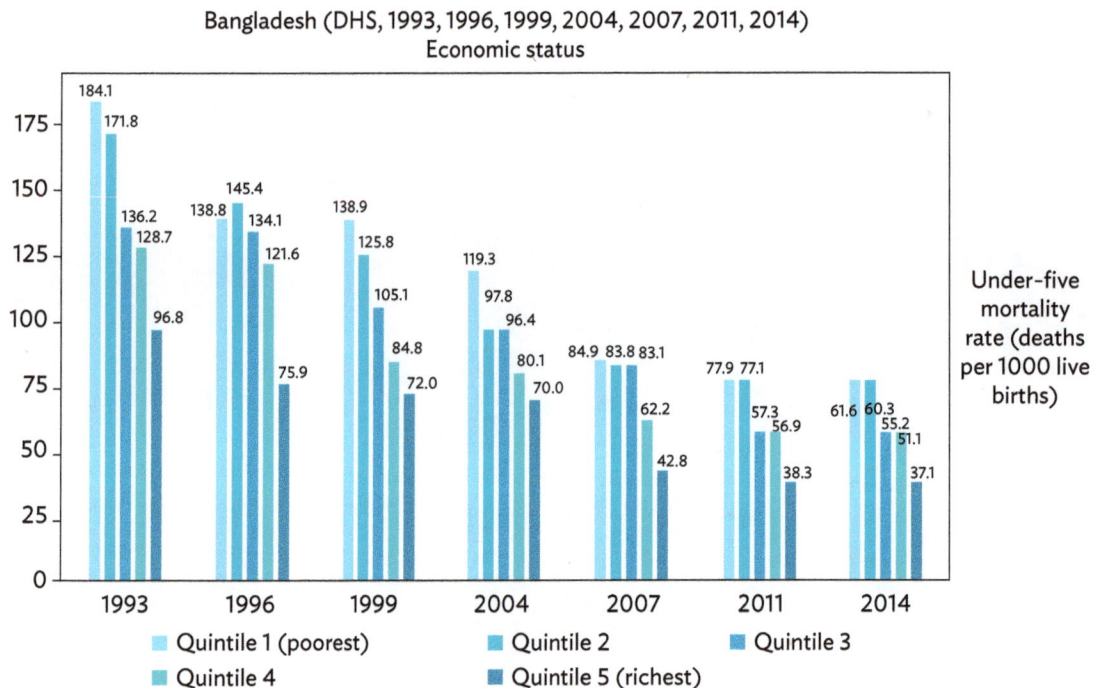

DHS = Demographic and Health Survey.
Source: Adapted from World Health Organization. Health Equity Assessment Toolkit: Built-in database edition, version 3.1. Available from https://whoequity.shinyapps.io/HEAT/ (accessed 9 March 2021).

In addition to inequality assessments based on disaggregated data, inequalities may also be assessed using summary measures of inequality. HEAT calculates up to 19 different summary measures of inequality, including both absolute and relative inequality measures. Absolute inequality measures indicate the magnitude of inequality in health between subgroups, while relative inequality measures show the proportional differences in health among subgroups.

For example, Figure 4.8 shows the difference in under-5 mortality rates between the richest and poorest quintiles in Bangladesh during 1993–2014, with a clear pattern of absolute inequality narrowing across time. In contrast, Figure 4.9 illustrates the ratio of under-5 mortality rates between the poorest and richest quintiles, showing that relative inequality fluctuated but changed little during the same year range. This example demonstrates the importance of analyzing both absolute and relative measures of inequality.

Figure 4.9: Ratio of Under-5 Mortality Rates among the Poorest and Richest Quintiles in Bangladesh, 1993–2014

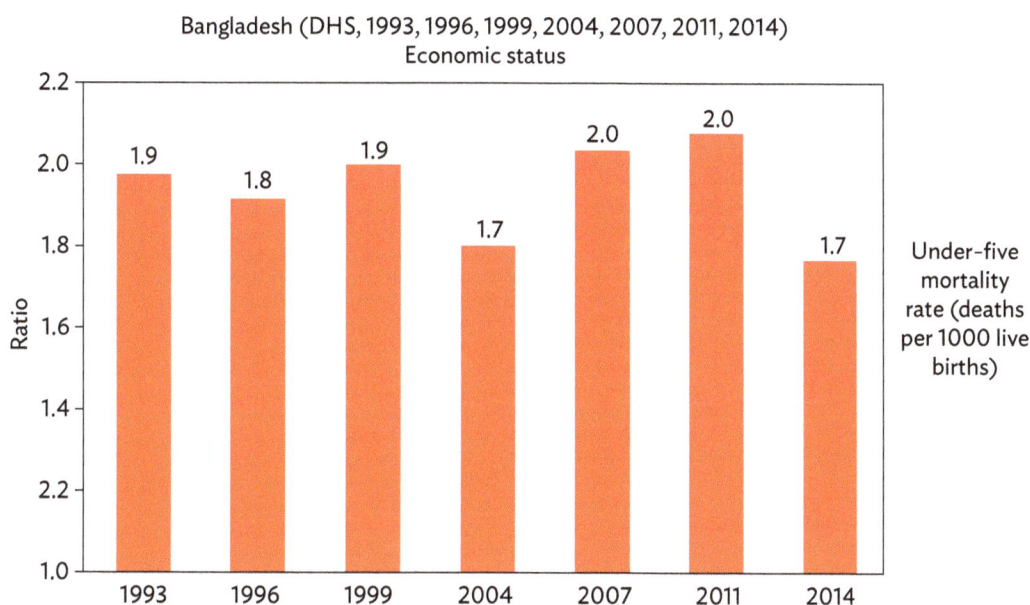

Bangladesh (DHS, 1993, 1996, 1999, 2004, 2007, 2011, 2014)
Economic status

DHS = Demographic and Health Survey.

Source: Adapted from World Health Organization. Health Equity Assessment Toolkit: Built-in database edition, version 3.1. Available from https://whoequity.shinyapps.io/HEAT/ (accessed 9 March 2021).

Aside from the difference and ratio measures, which are two simple measures of inequality that enable comparisons between two subgroups, HEAT also calculates complex measures of inequality, which take into account data from all subgroups to assess inequalities and provide a more nuanced picture. Absolute complex measures of inequality calculated in HEAT include the absolute concentration index, between-group standard deviation, between-group variance, population attributable risk, slope index of inequality, unweighted and weighted mean difference from the best performing subgroup, and unweighted and weighted mean difference from mean. Relative complex measures of inequality available in HEAT include the coefficient of variation, mean log deviation, population attributable fraction, relative concentration index, relative index of inequality, Theil index, and unweighted and weighted index of disparity. The Handbook on Health Inequality Monitoring published by WHO discusses in detail the measures used in calculating health inequalities.[67]

HEAT Plus, the upload database edition of the toolkit, has all the same features and functionalities as HEAT and it also allows users to upload and work with their own datasets. Databases have to be in a specific format to be uploaded to HEAT Plus, following the structure laid out in the HEAT Plus template. The flexibility of HEAT Plus makes it a suitable tool for equity assessments at the global, national, and subnational levels for a range of health and health-related indicators and inequality dimensions.

---

[67]   WHO. 2013. *Handbook on Health Inequality Monitoring: with a Special Focus on Low- and Middle-Income Countries.* Geneva. https://apps.who.int/iris/bitstream/handle/10665/85345/9789241548632_eng.pdf.

Recommended Reading

World Health Organization. *Health Equity Monitor.* http://www.who.int/gho/health_equity/en/.

The Health Equity Monitor serves as a platform for the Global Health Observatory health inequality database and theme page (containing interactive data visuals, country equity profiles, feature stories, analysis tools, and publications). Updated regularly, the Health Equity Monitor is a repository of disaggregated data from more than 100 primarily low- and middle-income countries.

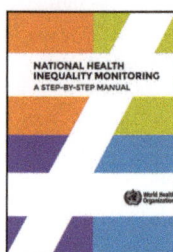

World Health Organization. 2017. *National Health Inequality Monitoring: A Step-by-Step Manual.* Geneva. https://apps.who.int/iris/bitstream/handle/10665/255652/9789241512183-eng.pdf.

This is a user-friendly resource, developed to help countries establish and strengthen health inequality monitoring practices. The handbook elaborates on the components of health inequality monitoring. Throughout the handbook, examples from low- and middle-income countries are presented to illustrate how concepts are relevant and applied in real-world situations. It is recognized in the 2014 British Medical Association Medical Book.

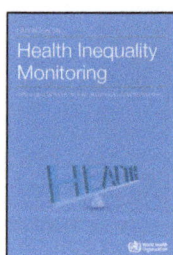

World Health Organization. 2013. *Handbook on Health Inequality Monitoring: with a Special Focus on Low- and Middle-Income Countries.* Geneva. https://apps.who.int/iris/bitstream/handle/10665/85345/9789241548632_eng.pdf.

This manual was designed as a highly accessible, practical reference to encourage and strengthen the practice of health inequality monitoring. The manual is organized according to a flow chart, which shows the steps and sub-steps of the health inequality monitoring cycle, with key questions and itemized checklists of data requirements, analysis and/or reporting activities, and/or decision points. While the manual focuses on health at the national level, the step-by-step approach may be applied to monitor inequalities within any defined population, ranging from a community context to a multinational context.

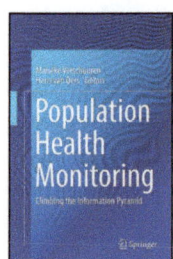

A.R. Hosseinpoor and N. Bergen. 2019. *Health Inequality Monitoring: A Practical Application of Population Health Monitoring.* In M. Verschuuren and H. van Oers, eds. Population Health Monitoring: Climbing the Information Pyramid. Springer: New York. https://link.springer.com/chapter/10.1007/978-3-319-76562-4_8.

This chapter draws from contemporary examples to illustrate one application of population monitoring: health inequality monitoring. It demonstrates how monitoring of health inequalities forms a central part of population health initiatives across global and national contexts. The primary aims of the chapter are to demonstrate the importance of health inequality monitoring for equity-oriented policies, programs, and practices; provide examples of how all steps of the health inequality monitoring cycle have been applied; discuss practical challenges of monitoring health inequalities; and suggest strategies for strengthening health inequality monitoring.

REPORTING, COMMUNICATING, AND IMPROVING USE OF DISAGGREGATED DATA

Overview

Disaggregating data to meet the leave no on behind (LNOB) principle is deemed meaningless if not translated to actual policy and program use. Policy advocates can capitalize on available disaggregated data on poverty that provide detailed information on who the poor are, where they live, how many they are, and why they are poor; this enables these advocates to speak on behalf of people experiencing severe socioeconomic disadvantage, and to make them visible in policy planning. An established Sustainable Development Goal (SDG) and national development plan data reporting system and effective dissemination platforms are thus imperative in ensuring that statistics on those disadvantaged by multiple or intersectional deprivations are accessed by and communicated to the target users, the implementers, and the general public.

This chapter highlights the data flows in the reporting of SDG data from national to international repositories and provides examples of indicator dashboards and in-country reporting mechanisms. It also discusses visualizations and dashboards on SDG statistics for ease of conveying patterns of inequities, and it presents a case study on how effective dissemination and communication of SDG statistics result in actual policy uses.

5.1   Reporting on Sustainable Development Goal Indicators

Global or Regional

Regular preparation of data and updates for the global indicators database on the SDGs requires a complex array of data flows, usually beginning with national data and statistics for global indicators by national statistics offices (NSOs) and other national data providers. The custodian agencies for the SDG indicators compile internationally comparable data and compute global indicators, informing countries when their data have been adjusted or estimated. Ultimately, the collation and reporting are done by the United Nations Statistics Division (UNSD).

Efficient and transparent transmission of country data, disaggregated data, and metadata for global SDG indicators can be facilitated if NSOs and custodian agencies adopt interoperable statistical data transmission standards, such as the Statistical Data and Metadata Exchange (SDMX).[68] SDMX can

---

[68]   UNSD. Inter-agency and Expert Group on SDG Indicators (IAEG-SDGs) Working Group on SDMX. https://unstats.un.org/sdgs/iaeg-sdgs/sdmx-working-group/.

be implemented in incremental steps, and used by non-technicians, but it cannot solve all the data validation challenges countries and custodian agencies face.

Guidelines on data flows and global data reporting for the SDGs have been prepared by the Inter-agency and Expert Group on SDG Indicators (IAEG-SDGs) and endorsed by the United Nations (UN) Statistical Commission.[69]

As part of its follow-up and review mechanisms, the 2030 Agenda for Sustainable Development encourages member states to "conduct regular and inclusive reviews of progress at the national and subnational levels, which are country-led and country-driven (footnote 1, p. 38)." These national reviews are presented as regular reviews by the UN High-level Political Forum on Sustainable Development (HLPF).[70] These regular reviews by the HLPF are voluntary, are state-led, are undertaken by both developed and developing countries, and involve multiple stakeholders.

The voluntary national reviews (VNRs) aim to facilitate the sharing of experiences, including successes, challenges, and lessons learned, with a view to accelerating the implementation of the 2030 Agenda. The VNRs also seek to strengthen policies and institutions of governments and to mobilize multi-stakeholder support and partnerships for the implementation of the SDGs.[71]

In-Country

In addition to preparing VNRs for SDG implementation, countries are disseminating and reporting national statistics on the SDGs through various media. The national SDG indicators do not only include the global SDG indicators available at the country level, but also proxy and supplementary indicators. Data for these national SDG indicators are made publicly available in their respective national reporting platforms, i.e., websites, databases, and associated information technology infrastructures for collecting, storing, securing, and ultimately disseminating data and related metadata and documentation in an easily accessible format. Target users of the national reporting platforms include government officials and policy makers, members of academic and research institutions, civil society organizations and other nongovernment and nonprofit organizations, development partners, media and other information providers, the private sector, and the general public.

Reporting on SDGs at the country level is dependent on institutional arrangements for statistical coordination, the legal framework that involves the sharing of data, and the understanding that data are a public good. A significant challenge, whether for country or global monitoring of the SDGs, is the availability of disaggregated data. A 2017 Asian Development Bank (ADB)-United Nations Economic and Social Commission for Asia and the Pacific (UN ESCAP) survey conducted in 22 countries revealed that among reporting economies, there is considerable disaggregation of statistics by location

---

[69] UNSD. IAEG-SDGs: *Improving data flows and global data reporting for the Sustainable Development Goals.* https://unstats.un.org/sdgs/iaeg-sdgs/data-flows/.

[70] UN. HLPF. https://sustainabledevelopment.un.org/hlpf.

[71] Various guides, as well as VNRs prepared by countries since 2018, are available here: UN HLPF VNRs. https://sustainabledevelopment.un.org/vnrs/.

for many SDG indicators.[72] However, data disaggregation is sparse for some indicators by sex, and even further limited—if not absent—for persons with disabilities and indigenous peoples. A 2018 report of ADB and the UN Entity for Gender Equality and the Empowerment of Women (UN Women) pointed out that of the 85 unique gender-related SDG indicators they examined, only 26% were available for more than two-thirds of the countries or territories in the Asia-Pacific region, while 41% had no relevant regional data.[73]

5.2 Communicating Data and Statistics on Sustainable Development Goals

Data Visualizations and Dashboards for Effectively Illustrating Inequities

An effective way to communicate data and statistics is through storytelling, made more meaningful with the use of visualizations.[74] Visualizations of disaggregated data clearly illustrate the inequalities across disaggregation dimensions and categories. They can make patterns easier to see or they can reveal patterns that might otherwise have been hidden.

When properly designed, visual information on disaggregation dimensions enables data exploration and effective storytelling that informs decision-making. The communication of data and statistics, including data visualization and storytelling, enables patterns in disaggregated data to be uncovered, understood, and communicated, especially for people facing multiple or intersectional deprivations (e.g., the proportion of working children in the poorest quintile in urban areas, or the proportion of children with access to safe water among the poorest quintile in rural areas).

For example, the spider chart (Figure 5.1) illustrates inequalities by displaying several indicators on reproductive health, education, decision-making, and access to finance in the form of a two-dimensional chart with the disaggregated data for the poorest rural Indian women and the corresponding richest Indian women in urban areas.

Graphs and historical charts in equity analysis tools such as the Health Equity Assessment Toolkit (HEAT) of the World Health Organization (WHO) described in Chapter 4 are particularly insightful for assessing gaps across disaggregation categories and examining disparities across time.

---

[72] Asian Development Bank and United Nations Economic and Social Commission for Asia and the Pacific. 2017. Survey on SDG Data Compilation.
[73] ADB and UN Women. 2018. *Gender Equality and the Sustainable Development Goals in Asia and the Pacific Baseline and pathways for transformative change by 2030.* Bangkok. https://www.adb.org/sites/default/files/publication/461211/gender-equality-sdgs-asia-pacific.pdf.
[74] UN Statistics Division (UNSD). Knowledgebase on Economic Statistics: Methods and Country Practices. UNECE "Making Data Meaningful" guide series: Parts 1, 2, and 3. https://unstats.un.org/unsd/EconStatKB/KnowledgebaseArticle10350.aspx.

Figure 5.1: Spider Chart Visualization of Multidimensional Inequalities

Inequalities between poorest rural and richest urban Indian women,
various indicators, percentage, 2015-2016

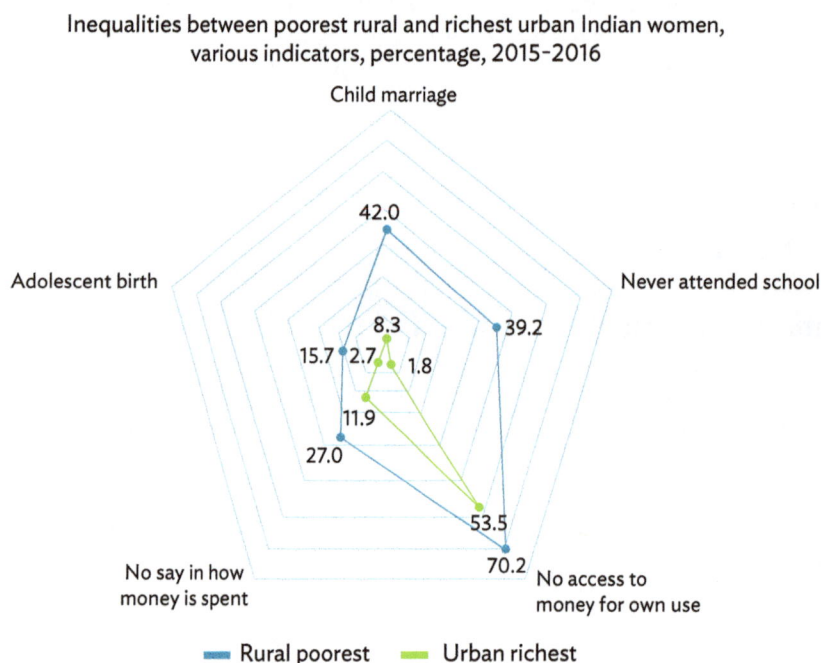

Source: Adapted from UN Women calculations based on micro-data from the India National Health Survey (NFHS-4/DHS).

Dashboards and Data Portals

Interactive visualizations and dashboards, such as the SDGs Interactive Dashboard (Figure 5.2) created by the social enterprise iTech Mission, show promise in helping citizens obtain snapshots of progress and challenges for attaining the SDGs. This dashboard tool makes use of data from the UN Global SDG Database in a way that allows users to explore and visualize data for analyzing SDG progress.[75] Users can assess their country's progress on the SDGs, and explore trends on a particular goal, target, or indicator using graphs, bubble or rank charts, tree maps, or tables. In addition, users can select and display SDG indicators using different metrics. A monitoring tool displays a given target and its indicators, and provides information on the data value, unit, and trend. Users can also view trends toward the achievement of targets, choose to track and monitor data on the SDGs that are most important to them, or create country profiles on the SDGs. The dashboard allows linking to the data from NSO and other government databases. A "citizens vote" tool is also available, which allows users to identify 6 (out of 16) issues that are most important to them, including access to a good education and action taken on climate change, and to see how their priorities compare with others across the world. The votes are recorded with the user's sex, age, education level, and location.

---

[75] UN Global SDG Database. https://unstats.un.org/sdgs/indicators/database/.

Figure 5.2: Features of the Sustainable Development Goals Global Dashboard

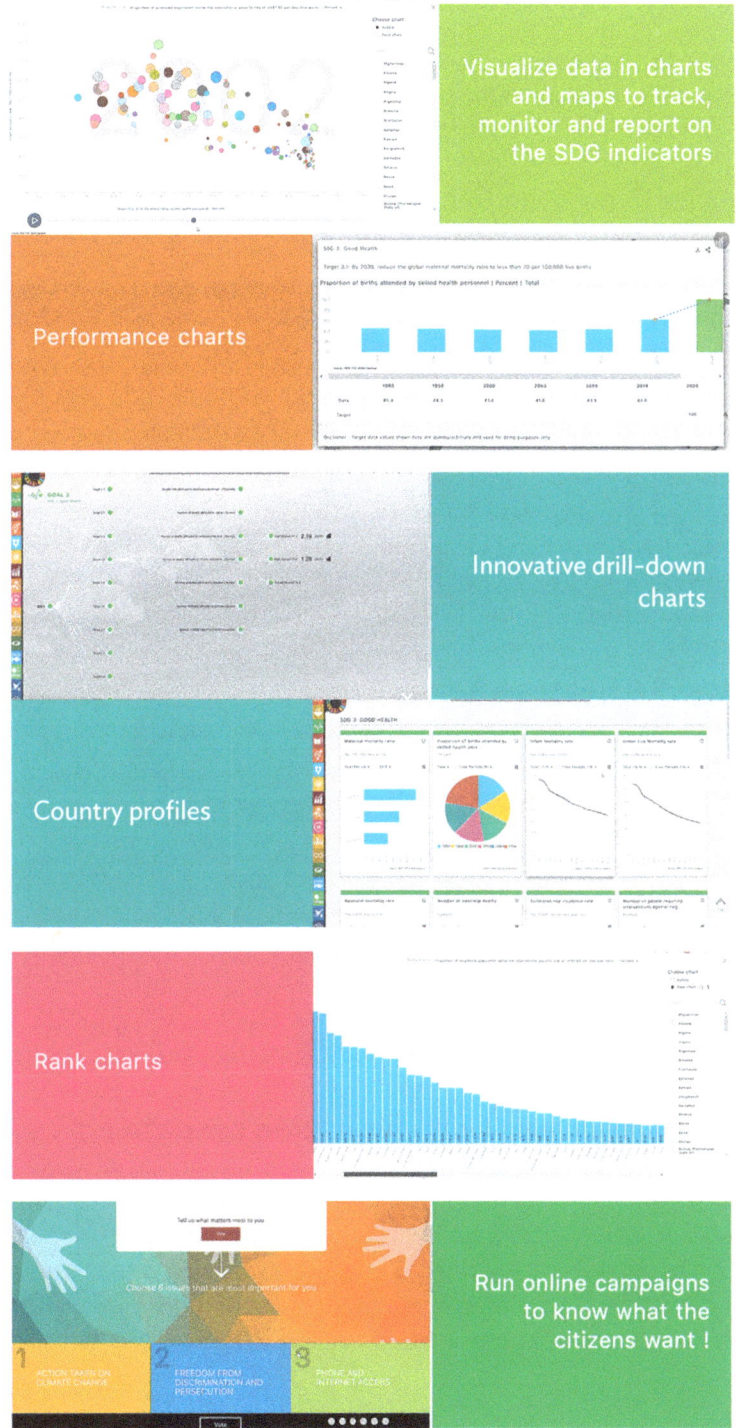

Source: Adapted from SDGs Global Dashboard. Available from https://www.sdgsdashboard.org.

Dashboards are linked to databases with the ability to pull real-time data from multiple sources and are designed to provide an at-a-glance view of vast amounts of information synthesized through graphs, indicators, symbols, and other visualization tools.

Countries are beginning to experiment using SDGs Global dashboard, with varying purposes and success.[76] Table 5.1 provides a list of data portals linked to the UNSD-Foreign, Commonwealth & Development Office (of the United Kingdom) Project on SDG Monitoring.[77]

Table 5.1: List of Sample Data Portals Linked to the United Nations Statistics Division-Foreign, Commonwealth & Development Office Project on Sustainable Development Goal Monitoring

Country	Link/Information
Bangladesh	Government of Bangladesh. SDG Tracker. http://www.sdg.gov.bd/
Burundi	Government of Burundi. Data Portal. https://burundi.opendataforafrica.org/addin/sdg
Cambodia	Government of Cambodia. National Indicator Reporting Platform. http://camstat.nis.gov.kh/#/
Ghana	Government of Ghana. Data for SDG Indicators. https://sustainabledevelopment-ghana.github.io/
Jordan	Government of Jordan. SDGs. Front end: http://dosweb.dos.gov.jo/sdgs/ Back end: http://jorinfo.dos.gov.jo/Databank/pxweb/en/SDG/
Kyrgyz Republic	Government of the Kyrgyz Republic. SDG Indicators. https://sustainabledevelopment-kyrgyzstan.github.io/
Mozambique	Government of Mozambique. SDGs. Partially online: https://mozambique.opendataforafrica.org/sdg
Rwanda	Government of Rwanda. Data for SDGs. https://sustainabledevelopment-rwanda.github.io/
Uganda	Government of Uganda. Data Portal. https://uganda.opendataforafrica.org/sdg
Zambia	Government of Zambia. Data Portal. http://zambia.opendataforafrica.org/addin/sdg
Zimbabwe	Government of Zimbabwe. Data Portal. https://zimbabwe.opendataforafrica.org/sdg

Notes: Additional details are found in UNSD's webpage.
Source: UNSD. UNSD-Foreign, Commonwealth & Development Office Project on SDG Monitoring. https://unstats.un.org/capacity-development/UNSD-FCDO/.

5.3   Improving Use of Results of Multilevel Analysis

How Effective Dissemination and Communication Leads to Policy Uses of Disaggregated Statistics: a Case Study

Access to granular data on poverty has a wide range of uses for socioeconomic planners and policy makers. Granular data on poverty that provide detailed information on who the poor are, where they live, how many they are, and why they are poor facilitate formulation of more efficient and effective strategies and programs on poverty reduction. These include social protection programs (including conditional

---

[76]   UN Development Programme. 2017. *SDG Dashboards: The role of information tools in the implementation of the 2030 Agenda.* http://www.asia-pacific.undp.org/content/dam/rbap/docs/meetTheSDGs/SDG Dashboards UNDP-SIGOB.pdf.
[77]   UNSD. UNSD- Foreign, Commonwealth & Development Office Project on SDG Monitoring. https://unstats.un.org/capacity-development/UNSD-FCDO/.

and non-conditional cash transfers), provision of unemployment benefits, employment facilitation, and tax reforms. Granular data on poverty can also be used to assess the impact of these programs over time.

The Philippine experience in collecting granular data on poverty is a good example showcasing a wide range of policy uses. The Philippine Statistics Authority conducts the triennial Family Income and Expenditure Survey (FIES), which is the main source of official poverty statistics. Until recently, FIES was designed to provide reliable estimates at the regional level. However, because of demand for more geographically disaggregated poverty statistics, since 2003, provincial poverty statistics have also been published, with a caveat for provinces with a large sampling error.[78] In 2005, the Philippine national statistical system (NSS) collaborated with the World Bank to undertake a poverty mapping project that resulted in the generation of municipality- and city-level poverty statistics using small area estimation (SAE) techniques. Since then, the Philippine Statistics Authority has updated the small area poverty estimates with the availability of new FIES rounds and the Census of Population and Housing.

Since municipality- and city-level poverty statistics became available in 2005, national and local government units in the Philippines have used the data as inputs for formulating and implementing poverty reduction programs. For example, the Government of the Philippines' Department of Social Welfare and Development had used the estimates to identify poor municipalities for data collection for its National Household Targeting System for Poverty Reduction (NHTS-PR), Kalahi-Comprehensive and Integrated Delivery of Social Services Program, assistance for families affected by typhoon Yolanda (Haiyan) in Western Visayas, Student Grants-in-Aid Program for Poverty Alleviation in the Cordillera Administrative Region, and Cash-for-Training Program in the SOCCSKSARGEN Region. The local government units of Negros Occidental and Pangasinan provinces; the municipality of Nabas in Aklan province; the city of Baguio; and the municipalities of La Trinidad, Itogon, Sablan, and Tuba in Benguet province also refer to the SAE as inputs for producing local socioeconomic profiles that aid in identifying areas requiring poverty intervention programs. The provincial governments of Aklan, La Union, Negros Occidental, Pangasinan, and Southern Leyte use the estimates in assessing the implementations of their poverty reduction programs. Further, international development organizations also use small area poverty estimates in various poverty-related alleviation programs in different areas in the country.[79]

In addition to the official poverty statistics (national, regional, and provincial) compiled by the Philippine Statistics Authority using data from FIES and municipal- and city-level poverty statistics compiled using the SAE technique, other government agencies have their own initiatives to collect granular data on poverty. For instance, the *Community-Based Monitoring System (CBMS)*, which was originally designed to provide policy makers and economic planners with a reliable information base that could be used for tracking the impacts of macroeconomic reforms and various policy shocks in the early 1990s, has evolved to include collection of disaggregated data that can be used for planning, program formulation, policy impact, and poverty monitoring. Since 2000, the CBMS has been adopted by local government units, and various government agencies have recognized the usefulness of the CBMS for various thematic concerns such as local planning, grassroots participatory budgeting, poverty diagnosis, monitoring of the Millennium Development Goals, disaster-risk reduction management and climate change adaptation,

---

[78] Starting in 2018, FIES adopted the Philippine Statistics Authority's 2013 Master Sample Design, with a sample size of about 180,000 sample households (i.e., four times the previous sample size). This significantly improved the reliability of provincial poverty statistics and allowed the generation of poverty statistics at the highly urbanized city level. Philippine Statistics Authority. 2019. 2018 Family Income and Expenditure Survey. https://psa.gov.ph/content/annual-family-income-estimated-php-313-thousand-average-2018.

[79] Philippine Statistics Authority. 2016. *2012 Municipal and City Level Poverty Estimates*. Manila. https://psa.gov.ph/sites/default/files/2012%20Municipal%20and%20City%20Level%20Poverty%20Estimates%20Publication%20%281%29_0.pdf.

gender and development, impact monitoring, and food insecurity. In 2019, the Government of the Philippines enacted the Community-Based Monitoring System Act to institutionalize the use of the CBMS as a tool for poverty alleviation program formulation and implementation.[80]

Furthermore, the National Household Targeting Office of the Department of Social Welfare and Development manages the NHTS-PR. The database identifies poor families, through a proxy means test, to estimate household income based on various social, economic, and housing characteristics. The database is accessible to national government agencies and other social protection stakeholders for identifying potential beneficiaries of social protection programs. The availability of such a database aims to minimize poorly targeted social services resulting from exclusions of the poor from necessary social services, which minimizes wastage of resources on those who are not actually poor. In 2020, when the Government of the Philippines launched the Social Amelioration Program in response to the coronavirus disease pandemic, the NHTS-PR was used to identify the poorest of the poor as target beneficiaries to receive cash grants.

Open Data Principles Increase Access to and Use of Disaggregated Data

Making use of aggregated and disaggregated data to inform policy and social good starts with open data principles, i.e., having data that are freely available online for anyone to use and republish for any purpose.[81] Aggregated (and disaggregated) data are typically the final products of NSOs and other data producers in an NSS; these are used to monitor trends in development and to inform public policy. Traditionally NSOs have disseminated aggregated and disaggregated data through yearbooks and publications (including censuses and sample survey reports). But with the rapid growth of the internet, most NSOs disseminate data and statistics on their websites. Further, using survey cataloguing software such as the World Bank's National Data Archive survey cataloguing software, several NSOs have also made micro-data—survey responses excluding identities of respondents to protect data privacy and confidentiality—available for public use.[82] Micro-data of surveys supported by the development community, such as the Demographic and Health Surveys (DHS), the Multiple Indicator Cluster Surveys (MICS), and the Living Standard Measurement Study (LSMS), are also available for public use (footnote 39). Data from the DHS and MICS are available for exploration and may be aggregated and disaggregated at different levels for examination over time and for cross-country comparison through platforms like STATcompiler[83] and MICS Compiler (footnote 39). When micro-data of the LSMS or other surveys that provide information on poverty are available, they can also be examined more systematically for generating aggregated and disaggregated statistics on poverty and inequality with the World Bank's software platform called the Automated Development Economics Poverty Tables (ADePT).[84]

[80] *Community-Based Monitoring System Act* (Republic Act No. 11315). 2018. https://www.officialgazette.gov.ph/downloads/2019/04apr/20190417-RA-11315-RRD.pdf.

[81] Open Data Watch. Open Data to Support Sustainable Development Goals. https://opendatawatch.com/publications/open-data-to-support-sustainable-development-goals/

[82] International Household Survey Network. National Data Archive survey cataloguing software. http://www.ihsn.org/projects/NADA-development.

[83] The DHS Program. https://www.statcompiler.com/en/.

[84] World Bank. ADePT. https://www.worldbank.org/en/topic/health/brief/adept-resource-center.

Recommended Reading

World Health Organization. Health Equity Assessment Toolkit (HEAT). https://www.who.int/data/gho/health-equity/assessment_toolkit.

HEAT is a software package that facilitates the assessment of within-country health inequalities. Users can create customized visuals based on disaggregated data or summary measures. There are two editions of the toolkit: (i) HEAT, the built-in database edition, which includes the World Health Organization Health Equity Monitor database; and (ii) HEAT Plus, the upload database edition, which allows users to upload and work with their own database.

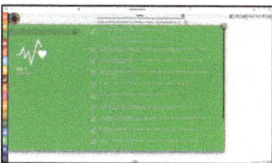

SDGs Global Dashboard. http://www.sdgsdashboard.org.

SDGs (Sustainable Development Goals) Interactive Dashboard is a platform that allows users to explore and visualize data to analyze progress. It uses data from the UN Statistics Division's SDG Database.

Users can monitor their country's progress on the SDGs Interactive Data Dashboard, explore trends on particular SDG indicators, and visualize the data in thematic maps, graphs, bubble or rank charts, tree maps or tables, among other outputs. The dashboard displays a given target and its indicators, and provides information on the data value, unit and trends.

PRODUCING AND USING DISAGGREGATED DATA— FROM POTENTIAL TO POSSIBLE

Overview

This final chapter looks at key issues on why required disaggregated data are often not available, and it provides information on knowledge products and ongoing capacity development initiatives that may help national statistical systems (NSSs) to address these issues.

6.1   Barriers to Producing and Using Disaggregated Data

Target 17.18 of the Sustainable Development Goals (SDGs) strongly and urgently recognizes that data and statistics, particularly disaggregated data, are crucial means of implementation for the goals.

> *By 2020, enhance capacity-building support to developing countries, including for least developed countries and small island developing States, to increase significantly the availability of high-quality, timely and reliable data disaggregated by income, gender, age, race, ethnicity, migratory status, disability, geographic location and other characteristics relevant in national contexts.*[85]

Available disaggregated data fall short of the data needs of the 2030 Agenda for Sustainable Development, especially because of a lack of resources and capacity. These challenges present opportunities for innovation to ensure that the SDGs become truly transformative and reach those furthest behind. Countries and the development community have a shared responsibility to ensure that NSSs are effective and capable of producing high-quality disaggregated data for monitoring the SDGs. This requires investments in human resources, new technologies, infrastructure, data architectures, geospatial data and management systems, and information intermediaries. Capacities for communicating data effectively must be developed to promote opportunities in improving data use that will contribute to ultimately attaining sustainable development. A 2018 survey showed that areas where support is needed for data disaggregation varied across regions (and countries) (Figure 6.1).

---

[85]   United Nations Statistics Division. SDG Indicators Metadata Repository. https://unstats.un.org/sdgs/metadata/?Text=&Goal=17 &Target=17.18.

Figure 6.1: Supporting the Monitoring of SDGs in Developing Countries: Priorities for Data Disaggregation

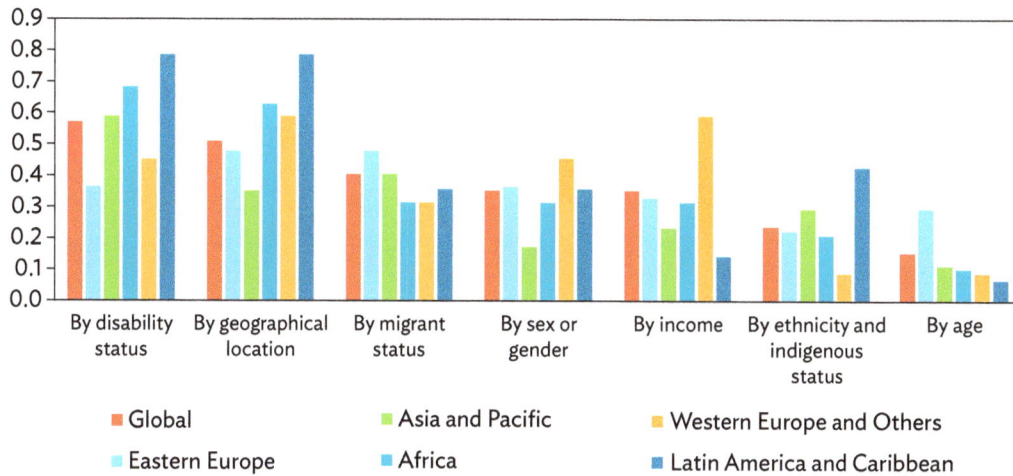

Source: Adapted from Partnership in Statistics for Development in the 21st Century and United Nations High-level Group for Partnership, Coordination and Capacity-Building for Statistics for the 2030 Agenda for Sustainable Development. 2018. *Survey Results: New Approaches to Capacity Development and Future Priorities*. Paris. Available from https://paris21.org/capacity-development-40/cd40-survey.

Apart from the technical challenges illustrated in the previous chapters, data governance issues relating to the human rights principle of "do no harm" need to be addressed, i.e., data collection exercises should not create or reinforce discrimination, bias, or stereotypes against population groups (Figure 6.2). Privacy, confidentiality, and data protection must be ensured, particularly for digit-based data (e.g., big data, geographic information system), for the more disaggregated or granular data collected, and for the (sometimes small) vulnerable populations where being visible may be harmful at the individual level.[86]

---

[86] These issues are addressed in United Nations (UN) Entity for Gender Equality and the Empowerment of Women (UN Women), UN Statistics Division (UNSD), and Intersecretariat Working Group on Household Surveys. 2020. *Concept Note and Agenda*. S. Badiee. 2020. Gender Data Governance and Official Statistics. Presentation prepared for Counted and Visible: Global conference on the measurement of gender equality and intersecting inequalities. New York. 26–27 February. https://data.unwomen.org/sites/default/files/documents/gender%20and%20intersecting%20inequalities/docs/presentations/2.8.1.%20Open%20data%20watch.pdf.

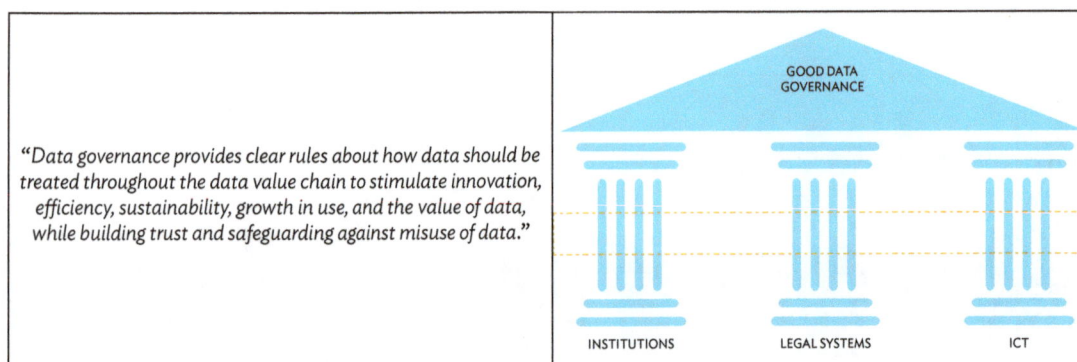

Figure 6.2: Definition of Data Governance

ICT = information and communication technology.
Source: Adapted from S. Badiee. 2020. *Gender Data Governance and Official Statistics*. Presentation prepared for Counted and Visible: Global conference on the measurement of gender equality and intersecting inequalities. New York. 26–27 February. Available from https://data.unwomen.org/sites/default/files/documents/gender%20and%20intersecting%20inequalities/docs/presentations/2.8.1.%20Open%20data%20watch.pdf.

6.2   Areas Where Capacity Development Is Needed

National statistics offices (NSOs) and development partners are exploring potential synergies and opportunities for collaboration to strengthen the "data for development" ecosystem. When using and integrating innovative data sources with traditional data sources in the statistical production system, NSOs are proceeding in steps, starting with clearly stating the focus of the analysis before consulting with data science experts and obtaining lessons from the experiences of other NSOs. Since such initiatives involve risks and experimentation, NSOs recognize the need for flexibility and patience in evaluating the potential for these innovations to meet the disaggregated data requirements of the SDGs in the context of the leave no one behind (LNOB) principle of the 2030 Agenda.

Improving Health Information Systems in Indonesia

Indonesia's approach in enhancing the equity orientation of its health information system highlighted in Box 6.1 illustrates capacity challenges and the processes that address them.

Zeroing in on Big Data

Making use of innovative data sources involves technological infrastructure spanning both hardware and software. Data analysis software tools may not be suitable or may not be efficiently used for large datasets in a sequential computer. NSOs need improved information communication and technology infrastructure to download big data (bandwidth), as well as to catalog, organize, and process big data in a sufficiently timely manner. The availability of interfaces by some statistical packages such as open source R and Hadoop MapReduce for most used statistical platforms, however, has significantly contributed to the use of big data analytics. A related technological issue is the curation of data, since big data results in a messy collage of data points whose accuracy is challenging to establish.

> ### Box 6.1: Enhancing the Equity Orientation of Health Information Systems: Indonesia
>
> Indonesia enhanced the equity orientation of its health information system through capacity building activities undertaken by the World Health Organization (WHO) from April 2016 to December 2017. This involved a series of workshops, meetings, and processes on health inequality monitoring, including identifying health topics or areas of interest, mapping data sources and identifying gaps, conducting equity analyses using raw datasets, and interpreting and reporting inequality results. As a result of these activities, WHO and Indonesia's Ministry of Health jointly produced the first national report on the state of health inequality. Sustained political will across various levels of administration and leadership is the main reason for the progress of health inequality monitoring in the country. Challenges experienced during the process highlighted the need for (i) the availability of raw datasets; (ii) active collaboration across various government units; (iii) further capacity building in quantitative and qualitative research methods; and (iv) routine inclusion of dimensions of inequality in surveys, civil registration, health facilities, and other relevant data sources through a consensus across government agencies to include priority dimensions of inequality. This capacity building for health inequality monitoring exercise in Indonesia is adaptable to other contexts.
>
> Source: WHO. 2017. *State of Health Inequality: Indonesia.* Geneva. https://www.who.int/gho/health_equity/report_2017_indonesia/en/.

While NSOs have experience in curating data, many have no data scientists who have a strong data and computational focus. NSOs and other data producers are also recognizing the need for new legal protocols and institutional arrangements to access big data holdings for development purposes, as well as to prevent the misuse of big data.

While big data has been customarily characterized to have three Vs—(large) volume, velocity, and variety—big data is not just about collecting incidental data (what some call "digital bread crumbs" or "digital exhaust"), but also about capacities, including econometric tools, software, and hardware for uncovering patterns and the community or data ecosystem. Harnessing data from innovative data sources such as geospatial information, earth observations, mobile data, social media, and/or crowd-sourced data with those from traditional data sources requires data interoperability, which is the ability to (i) access and process data assets from multiple sources and multiple formats without losing meaning, and (ii) integrate these assets into coherent information products or services (e.g., for mapping, visualization, and other forms of analysis).[87]

---

[87]   L. Morales and T. Orrell. 2019. *Data Interoperability: A Practitioner's Guide to Joining up Data in the Development Sector.* https://www.data4sdgs.org/sites/default/files/services_files/Interoperability%20-%20A%20practitioner's%20guide%20to%20joining-up%20data%20in%20the%20development%20sector.pdf.

Readiness for Use of Big Data in Official Statistics: Addressing Barriers through Training[88]

Barriers

Key point 1—Strategic coordination: Only one-third of all NSOs have overarching big data strategies in place, and not all NSOs have chief data officers. The biggest challenge for NSOs is collaboration with big data source owners outside the government.

Key point 2—Legal frameworks: These frameworks are still insufficient to regulate big data applications. Only a small share of NSOs rely on legal frameworks that guarantee access to big data.

Key point 3—Information technology infrastructure: This infrastructure is a central barrier to developing big data capacity, and many NSOs need to improve their on-site and off-site storage capacity. Only a few NSOs consider cloud storage a relevant option.

Key point 4—Human resources: Most NSOs lack a competency framework to develop new skills to cope with big data (e.g., mobile phone, geospatial data) and new methodologies (e.g., machine learning).

Training on Big Data[89]

The different barriers in generating big data discussed above impose immense pressure on official statistics, since their role in ensuring the highest standards and quality of statistical information becomes even more vital in the era of fake news and post-truth. In addition, official statistics are expected to keep up with the growing demands of data users. To this end, attempts to modernize statistical production have been increasingly undertaken by NSOs, since they recognize the potential of novel data processing techniques and new data sources. With regard to these new data sources, big data have been of particular interest to NSOs. Yet they entail other challenges, not only at the level of their acquisition and implementation into the statistical production, but also in the realm of sustaining relevant skills that reach beyond the traditional set of statistical competencies. To address these challenges, the United Nations (UN) Global Working Group on Big Data for Official Statistics' Task Team on Training, Competencies and Capacity Development has developed a competency framework for use by NSOs. It covers the wide array of skills and knowledge considered relevant for those working with big data acquisition and processing. The proposed framework involves core competencies, as well as a more general set of soft skills (Figure 6.3).

---

[88]   UN Global Working Group Task Team on Training, Competencies and Capacity Development. 2020. *Global assessment of institutional readiness for the use of big data in official statistics.* https://unstats.un.org/bigdata/task-teams/training/UN_BigData_report_v5.0.html.

[89]   UN Global Working Group on Big Data. *Training, Competencies and Capacity Development.* https://unstats.un.org/bigdata/task-teams/training/index.cshtml.

Figure 6.3: Big Data-Related Competencies

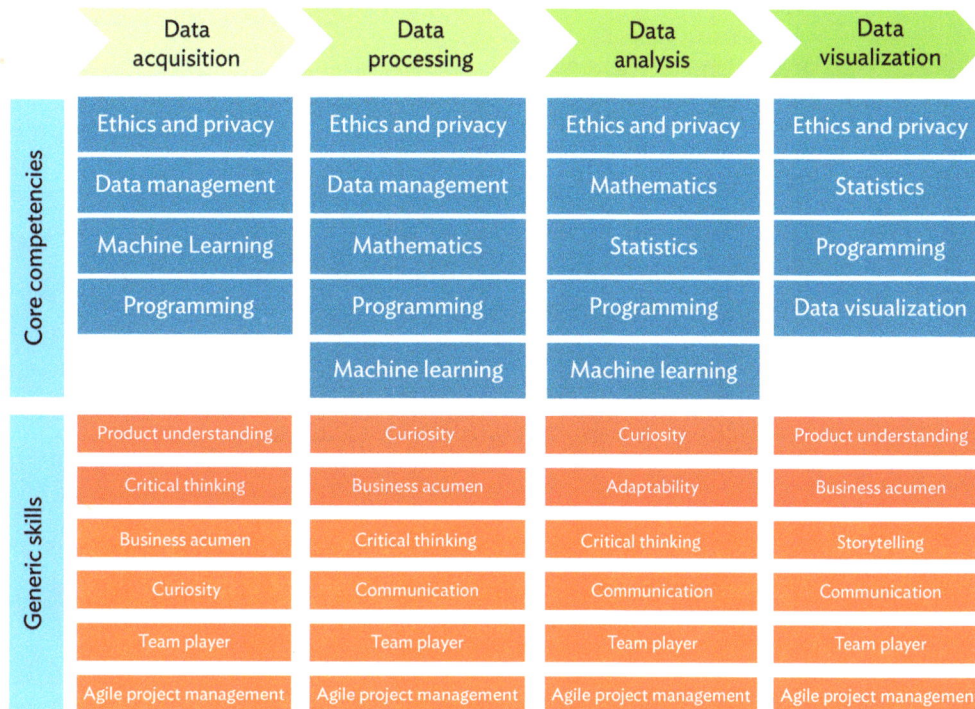

	Data acquisition	Data processing	Data analysis	Data visualization
Core competencies	Ethics and privacy	Ethics and privacy	Ethics and privacy	Ethics and privacy
	Data management	Data management	Mathematics	Statistics
	Machine Learning	Mathematics	Statistics	Programming
	Programming	Programming	Programming	Data visualization
		Machine learning	Machine learning	
Generic skills	Product understanding	Curiosity	Curiosity	Product understanding
	Critical thinking	Business acumen	Adaptability	Business acumen
	Business acumen	Critical thinking	Critical thinking	Storytelling
	Curiosity	Communication	Communication	Communication
	Team player	Team player	Team player	Team player
	Agile project management	Agile project management	Agile project management	Agile project management

Source: Adapted from United Nations Global Working Group on Big Data for Official Statistics' Task Team on Training, Competencies and Capacity Development. 2020. *Competency Framework for Big Data Acquisition and Processing.* Available from https://unstats.un.org/bigdata/task-teams/training/UNGWG_Competency_Framework.pdf.

6.3   Investing in Disaggregated Data

Despite the importance of having disaggregated information, there are several reasons why official statistics are usually expressed as aggregated data. Budget constraints are foremost. In some cases, the vulnerable groups are hard to capture in conventional data collection systems. For instance, people living on the streets may not necessarily be covered in household surveys because they are not included in sampling frames. It is also difficult to get data from people living in very remote and/or conflict areas, even if financial resources to collect data on these groups are available. Additionally, in cases where resources might be sufficient, many policy makers are more comfortable with tracking a limited number of aggregate figures than studying a more complex array of information disaggregated across multiple dimensions. For this reason, the development of new methods and increased affordability of statistical disaggregation tools must be accompanied by new techniques for communication of these statistics via dashboards and other communication tools so that non-statisticians can grasp their meaning and importance for policy formulation, implementation, and monitoring.

Box 6.2: What This Means: Statistics Canada

In 2018/2019, the Government of Canada allocated Can$6.7 million in funding over 5 years, with Can$600,000 thereafter, to create the Centre for Gender, Diversity and Inclusion Statistics. The goal of the center is to support evidence-based policy and program development by monitoring and reporting on gender, diversity, and inclusion. In addition to this funding, Statistics Canada received Can$4.2 million in 2019/2020 for four distinct activities, as part of Canada's anti-racism strategy. Statistics Canada continues to work with its federal, provincial, and territorial counterparts to develop ways to paint a more complete picture of the situation.

Source: Government of Canada, Statistics Canada. Transparency and accountability. Statistics Canada and disaggregated data. https://www.statcan.gc.ca/eng/transparency-accountability/disaggregated-data.

Global Initiatives: The Cape Town Global Action Plan for Sustainable Development Data

A systematic way of building capacity and mobilizing the needed resources to do so has been mapped out in the Cape Town Global Action Plan for Sustainable Development Data.[90] Of particular relevance to disaggregated data is objective 3.5 of the plan (Figure 6.4).

Figure 6.4: Objective 3.5 of the Cape Town Global Action Plan for Sustainable Development Data

Objective 3.5: Strengthen and expand data on all groups of population to ensure that no one is left behind.

Key Actions:

- Improve the production of high-quality, accessible, timely, reliable and disaggregated data by all characteristics relevant in national contexts to ensure that no one is left behind.
- Promote the systematic mainstreaming of gender equality in all phases of planning production and usage of data and statistics.
- Support the strengthening and further development of methodology and standards for disability statistics.
- Promote the expansion of data collection programmes to ensure the coverage of all age groups.

Source: Adapted from UN High-level Group for Partnership, Coordination and Capacity-Building for Statistics for the 2030 Agenda for Sustainable Development. 2017. *Cape Town Global Action Plan for Sustainable Development Data*. Available from https://unstats.un.org/sdgs/hlg/Cape-Town-Global-Action-Plan/.

---

[90] UN High-level Group for Partnership, Coordination and Capacity-Building for Statistics for the 2030 Agenda for Sustainable Development. 2017. *Cape Town Global Action Plan for Sustainable Development Data*. https://unstats.un.org/sdgs/hlg/Cape-Town-Global-Action-Plan/.

The plan also highlights the importance of new technologies and data sources that have been discussed in this guidebook (Figure 6.5).

Figure 6.5: Objective 2.3 of the Cape Town Global Action Plan for Sustainable Development Data

Objective 2.3: Facilitate the application of new technologies and new data sources into mainstream statistical activities.

Key Actions:

- Identify specifications for interoperable, open source technologies to incorporate the flexibility in information systems needed to allow the strategic use of new and emerging technologies for official data collection, processing, dissemination and analysis.

- Identify and remove barriers to the use of new data sources, including registries and administrative data and other data from new and innovative sources, and coordinate efforts to incorporate them into mainstream statistical programmes through, inter alia, confidence-and trust-building measures, legal reforms, better funding and capacity building.

- Develop guidelines on the use of new and innovative data generated outside the official statistical system, into official statistics (that is, principles on using new data sources and other data for official statistics).

- Promote the development of integrated database systems to support the efficient and effective review and follow-up of the implementation process of the 2030 Agenda for Sustainable Development, building, where possible, on existing MDG database platforms.

Source: Adapted from UN High-level Group for Partnership, Coordination and Capacity-Building for Statistics for the 2030 Agenda for Sustainable Development. 2017. *Cape Town Global Action Plan for Sustainable Development Data.* Available from https://unstats.un.org/sdgs/hlg/Cape-Town-Global-Action-Plan/.

Exploring Other Data Sources: Citizen-Generated Data

With respect to new data sources and other data, ***citizen-generated data (CGD)*** as a source is increasingly being explored by NSSs. A plethora of concepts and initiatives use CGD to achieve many goals, including citizen science, citizen sensing, environmental monitoring, participatory mapping, community-based monitoring, and community policing. In these initiatives, citizens may play very different roles, including taking on the role of mere sensors or shaping what data gets collected. Initiatives may differ in respect to the media and technologies used to collect data, the ways stakeholders are engaged with partners from government or business, and how activities are governed to align interests between these parties.[91]

---

[91] Global Partnership for Sustainable Development Data. 2019. Resources. *Choosing and engaging with citizen-generated data: A guide.* https://www.data4sdgs.org/resources/choosing-and-engaging-citizen-generated-data-guide.

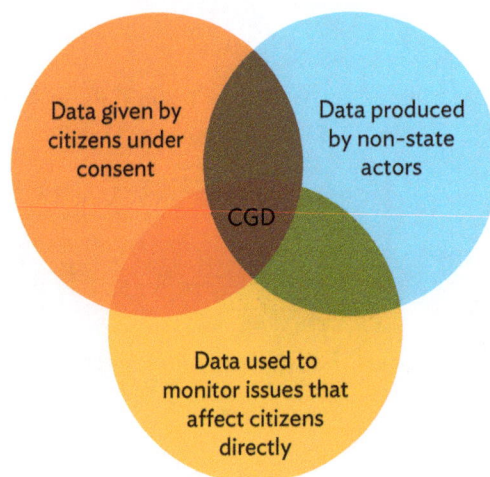

Figure 6.6: What Is Citizen-Generated Data?

Data given by citizens under consent

Data produced by non-state actors

CGD

Data used to monitor issues that affect citizens directly

CGD = citizen-generated data.
Source: Adapted from Partnership in Statistics for Development in the 21st Century. *Citizen-Generated Data*. Available from https://paris21.org/cgd.

Using citizen-generated data requires capacities and processes that NSOs need to consider and learn. These are outlined in the Global Partnership for Sustainable Development Data's *Choosing and engaging with citizen-generated data* (footnote 91).

Country explorations on CGD initiatives are documented below:

(i)   Philippines: PARIS21. 2020. New report shares insights on using citizen-generated data for SDG reporting in the Philippines. News release. 4 August. https://paris21.org/news-center/news/new-report-shares-insights-using-citizen-generated-data-sdg-reporting-philippines.

(ii) Maldives: PARIS21. 2020. Citizen-generated gender data in Maldives: connecting data ecosystems. News release. 10 June. https://paris21.org/news-center/news/citizen-generated-gender-data-maldives-connecting-data-ecosystems.

6.4   Systematic Assessment and Approach to Capacity Development

Integrating Gender in National Strategies for the Development of Statistics

National strategies for the development of statistics (NSDS) are the key instrument for communicating visions for improving data and statistics and systematically mobilizing resources. As part of its collaboration with the United Nations (UN) Entity for Gender Equality and the Empowerment of Women (UN Women), PARIS21 developed a comprehensive framework to assess data and capacity gaps linked to gender statistics.[92] The framework, aimed at NSOs, proposes methods, activities, and tools for conducting assessments related to gender statistics to support the mainstreaming of gender statistics in NSSs. The assessment report resulting from the application of this framework is meant to inform NSDS.[93]

Capacity Development 4.0

PARIS21 has launched a pioneering approach to capacity development—Capacity Development 4.0— that goes beyond technical skills and emphasizes leadership, change management, advocacy, and networking (Figure 6.7).[94] This approach constitutes the first guidelines (and a road map) to advise NSOs and development cooperation agencies on how to engage in country-led, sustainable, and participative statistical capacity development. The guidelines explain the Capacity Development 4.0 approach and present 30 activities on how to implement capacity development program, illustrated by case studies to provide real-world context.

Box 6.3: Making Gender Statistics a Top Priority in the Senegalese National Strategy for the Development of Statistics

"Following an 8-months-long process, Senegal adopted its third national strategy for development of statistics (NSDS III) for 2019–2023 with the support of the African Development Bank and PARIS21. One of the most remarkable features of this strategy is the plan to expand the production and dissemination of gender statistics at the national level. This goal constitutes the first strategic pillar of the NSDS III, and aims to make official gender statistics more responsive to increasing demand."

Source: Partnership in Statistics for Development in the 21st Century. 2020. *Making Gender Statistics a Top Priority in the Senegalese National Strategy for Development of Statistics*. News release. 11 March. https://paris21.org/news-center/news/making-gender-statistics-top-priority-senegalese-national-strategy-development.

---

[92] PARIS21. Supporting Gender Statistics. https://paris21.org/supporting-gender-statistics.
[93] PARIS21. NSDS Guidelines. https://nsdsguidelines.paris21.org/; PARIS21 and UN Women. 2020. *Assessing Data and Statistical Capacity Gaps for Better Gender Statistics: Framework and Implementation Guidelines*. https://paris21.org/sites/default/files/inline-files/Framework%202020_update_web_0.pdf; PARIS21 and UN Women. Forthcoming. *Guidelines for Integrating Gender in National Strategies for Sustainable Development*.
[94] PARIS21. 2020. *Guidelines for Developing Statistical Capacity: A Roadmap for Capacity Development 4.0*. https://paris21.org/sites/default/files/inline-files/UNV003_Guidelines%20for%20Capacity%20Development%20PRINT_0.pdf.

Figure 6.7: Framework of Capacity Development 4.0

Target/Level	Individual	Organizational	System
Resources			
	• Professional background	• Human resources • Budget • Infrastructure	• Legislation, principles and institutional setting • Funds infrastructure • Plans (NSDS, sectoral...) • Existing data
Skills and knowledge			
	• Technical skills • Work know-how • Problem solving and creative thinking	• Statistical production processes • Quality assurance and codes of conduct • Innovation • Communication	• Data literacy • Knowledge sharing
Management			
	• Time management and prioritization • Leadership	• Strategic planning and monitoring and evaluation • Organizational design • HR management • Change management • Fundraising strategies	• NSS coordination mechanisms • Data ecosystem co-ordination • Advocacy strategy
Politics and power			
	• Teamwork and collaboration • Communication and negotiation skills • Strategic networking	• Transparency • Workplace politics	• Relationship between producers • Relationship with users • Relationship with political authorities • Relationship with data providers • Accountability
Incentives			
	• Career expectations • Income and social status • Work ethic and self-motivation	• Compensation and benefits • Organizational culture • Reputation	• Stakeholder interests • Political support • Legitimacy

HR = human resources, NSDS = national strategies for the development of statistics, NSS = national statistical system.

Source: Adapted from Partnership in Statistics for Development in the 21st Century. 2020. *Guidelines for Developing Statistical Capacity: A Roadmap for Capacity Development 4.0.* Available from https://paris21.org/sites/default/files/inline-files/UNV003_Guidelines%20for%20Capacity%20Development%20PRINT_0.pdf.

Challenges of Data Disaggregation and Options for Improvement—Assessment, Use of Advance Data Planning Tool (ADAPT), Examining Options for Improvement and Integrating into NSDS— Country Experiences

(i)   Cambodia: Government of Cambodia, National Institute of Statistics. 2019. *Cambodia Experience in Producing Disaggregated Data for SDGs.* Presentation prepared for the International Workshop on Data Disaggregation for the SDGs. Bangkok. 28–30 January. https://unstats.un.org/sdgs/files/meetings/sdg-inter-workshop-jan-2019/Session%20 2.b.1_Cambodia_Experience%20in%20producing%20disaggregated%20data%20 for%20SDGs.pdf.

(ii)   Ethiopia: Government of Ethiopia, Central Statistical Agency. 2019. *Data Disaggregation Practice on National SDG Implementation in Ethiopia.* Presentation prepared for the International Workshop on Data Disaggregation for the SDGs. Bangkok. 28–30 January. https://unstats.un.org/sdgs/files/meetings/sdg-inter-workshop-jan-2019/Session%20 2.b.2_%20Ethiopia%20Data%20Disaggregation%20Practice%20on%20National%20 SDG.pdf.

(iii) Turkmenistan: Government of Turkmenistan, State Committee of Turkmenistan on Statistics. 2019. *Data Disaggregation for SDGs: Turkmenistan's Experience.* Presentation prepared for the International Workshop on Data Disaggregation for the SDGs. Bangkok. 28–30 January. https://unstats.un.org/sdgs/files/meetings/sdg-inter-workshop-jan-2019/ Session%202.b.3_Turkmenistan_Bang_270119%20ENG%20PRINT.pdf.

What's Next

This guidebook has two versions—a printed publication and an online version that will be a "living document" continually updated to keep up with the growing work and experiences that generate useful knowledge for producing and analyzing data to LNOB. For example, the following important knowledge products were not available during the preparation of this guidebook:

(i)   *Draft Compilation of tools/guidance of existing materials for data disaggregation*[95]

This compilation is prepared by the Inter-agency and Expert Group on SDG Indicators (IAEG-SDGs) and UN Statistics Division (UNSD) based on a stock-taking questionnaire to established city and expert groups under the United Nations Statistical Commission (UNSC), international expert groups or committees, as well as UN agencies and stakeholders focusing on vulnerable populations, disaggregation dimensions, and data collection methods.

---

[95] IAEG-SDGs and UNSD. Forthcoming. *Compilation of tools/guidance of existing materials for data disaggregation.* https://unstats.un.org/unsd/statcom/52nd-session/documents/BG-3a-Compilation_of_tools_and_resources_for_data_ disaggregation-E.pdf.

(ii)   *Counted and Visible: Toolkit to Better Utilize Existing Household Surveys to Generate Disaggregated Gender Statistics.*[96]

The toolkit is a collection of good practices and lessons from select country studies, each focusing on specific aspects of the statistical process aimed at ensuring a holistic, sustainable, and institutionalized approach of producing disaggregated gender statistics using existing data from household surveys. The toolkit covers five major stages promoting capacity development of NSSs, particularly NSOs throughout the process. The five stages were also guided by the overarching aims of UN Women's global gender data program, Women Count, of ensuring an enabling environment, increasing data production, and increasing access and use to inform policies.

[96]   UN Women and Intersecretariat Working Group on Household Surveys. 2021. *Counted and Visible: Toolkit to Better Utilize Existing Household Surveys to Generate Disaggregated Gender Statistics.* https://data.unwomen.org/resources/counted-and-visible-toolkit.

APPENDIX: ONLINE RESOURCES FROM WORKSHOPS ON SUSTAINABLE DEVELOPMENT GOAL DISAGGREGATION

International Workshop on Data Disaggregation for SDGs, 28–30 January 2019, Bangkok
https://unstats.un.org/sdgs/meetings/sdg-inter-workshop-jan-2019/

Topic/Area	Online Resource
Overview of data disaggregation for the Sustainable Development Goals (SDGs), assessments, general approaches	United Nations Statistics Division (UNSD). Data Disaggregation and the Global Indicator Framework. https://unstats.un.org/sdgs/files/meetings/sdg-inter-workshop-jan-2019/Session%202.a_UNSD%20IAEG.pdf.
	UNSD. Cambodia Experience in Producing Disaggregated Data for SDGs. https://unstats.un.org/sdgs/files/meetings/sdg-inter-workshop-jan-2019/Session%202.b.1_Cambodia_Experience%20in%20producing%20disaggregated%20data%20for%20SDGs.pdf.
	UNSD. Data Disaggregation Practice on National SDG Implementation in Ethiopia. https://unstats.un.org/sdgs/files/meetings/sdg-inter-workshop-jan-2019/Session%202.b.2_%20Ethiopia%20Data%20Disaggregation%20Practice%20on%20National%20SDG.pdf.
	UNSD. Data Disaggregation for SDGs: Turkmenistan's Experience. https://unstats.un.org/sdgs/files/meetings/sdg-inter-workshop-jan-2019/Session%202.b.3_Turkmenistan_Bang_270119%20ENG%20PRINT.pdf.
	UNSD. Data Disaggregation for SDGs: United Kingdom. https://unstats.un.org/sdgs/files/meetings/sdg-inter-workshop-jan-2019/Session%202.b.4_UK_DataDisagregation_ONS_DFID.pdf.
Integrating policy demands on inclusive development with data	UNSD. Human Rights-Based Approach to Data. https://unstats.un.org/sdgs/files/meetings/sdg-inter-workshop-jan-2019/Session%203.a_OHCHR%20HRBAD%20data%20disaggregation.FINAL.pdf.
	UNSD. Every Policy Is Connected (EPIC): A Tool for Policy-Data Integration. https://unstats.un.org/sdgs/files/meetings/sdg-inter-workshop-jan-2019/Session%203.b_ESCAP_Data%20Disaggregation_Jan2019.pdf.
	UNSD. EPIC Case Study—Samoa: Education Sector. https://unstats.un.org/sdgs/files/meetings/sdg-inter-workshop-jan-2019/Session%203.c.1_Samoa_Presentation_5.pdf.
	UNSD. EPIC Case Study—Philippines: Women's Economic Empowerment. https://unstats.un.org/sdgs/files/meetings/sdg-inter-workshop-jan-2019/Session%203.c.2_%20Philippines%20Presentation_EPIC.pdf.
Sources: Censuses and household surveys	UNSD. Using Census for Producing Disaggregated Data. https://unstats.un.org/sdgs/files/meetings/sdg-inter-workshop-jan-2019/Session%206.a_CensusDisaggr-UNSD.pdf.
	UNSD. United Nations Children's Fund (UNICEF): Producing Disaggregated Data from Household Surveys (Highlighting MICS). https://unstats.un.org/sdgs/files/meetings/sdg-inter-workshop-jan-2019/Session%206.b_UNICEF_DA%20Data%20Disaggregation%20Bangkok%20Jan%202019.pdf.

Topic/Area	Online Resource
	UNSD. Mexico: Household Surveys for Producing Disaggregated Data. https://unstats.un.org/sdgs/files/meetings/sdg-inter-workshop-jan-2019/Session%206.c.1_Household%20survey%20data_MexicanCase_29Jan2019.pdf.
	UNSD. Ghana: Ghana's Experience (utilizing various data sources). https://unstats.un.org/sdgs/files/meetings/sdg-inter-workshop-jan-2019/Session%206.c.2_Ghana_DataDisaggregation_Thailand_Gh_28012019.pdf.
Sources: Administrative data	UNSD. Use of Administrative Sources for Producing Disaggregated Data (Highlighting Challenges). https://unstats.un.org/sdgs/files/meetings/sdg-inter-workshop-jan-2019/Session%205.a_UNSD.pdf.
	UNSD. Republic of Korea: Examples of General Initiatives and Challenges. https://unstats.un.org/sdgs/files/meetings/sdg-inter-workshop-jan-2019/Session%205.b.1_Korea%20Using%20administrative%20data_KOSTAT.pdf.
	UNSD. Rwanda: Using Administrative Data Sources for Producing Disaggregated Data (Highlighting Administrative Systems. Potential Uses and Challenges). https://unstats.un.org/sdgs/files/meetings/sdg-inter-workshop-jan-2019/Session%205.b.2_Rwanda_presentation_administrative_data_for_sdgs.pdf.
Sources: Small area estimation (SAE)	UNSD. Asian Development Bank (ADB): Small Area Estimation and Big Data (Theory and Illustrations of SAE). https://unstats.un.org/sdgs/files/meetings/sdg-inter-workshop-jan-2019/Session%207.a_ADB_Small%20Area%20Estimation%20-%20jan29.pdf.
	UNSD. Thailand: Illustrating Poverty Mapping. https://unstats.un.org/sdgs/files/meetings/sdg-inter-workshop-jan-2019/Session%207.c.1_Country%20Presentation%20Thailand.pdf.
	UNSD. Philippines: Efforts in Monitoring SDG with Disaggregation. https://unstats.un.org/sdgs/files/meetings/sdg-inter-workshop-jan-2019/Session%207.c.3_SAE%20Presentation%20Philippines_29January2019%20rev.pdf.
	UNSD. Indonesia: Small Area Estimation Study for Providing and Disaggregating SDGs Indicators. https://unstats.un.org/sdgs/files/meetings/sdg-inter-workshop-jan-2019/Session%207.c.2_Indonesia-SAE%20for%20Data%20Dissagregassion-January2019.pdf.
Sources: Big data	UNSD. ADB: Small Area Estimation and Big Data. https://unstats.un.org/sdgs/files/meetings/sdg-inter-workshop-jan-2019/Session%207.a_ADB_Small%20Area%20Estimation%20-%20jan29.pdf.
Inequality and leave no one behind (LNOB) analysis: Gender equality and multiple deprivation assessment	UNSD. United Nations Entity for Gender Equality and the Empowerment of Women (UN Women): Gender Data and Multilevel Disaggregation: an LNOB Perspective to SDG Monitoring. https://unstats.un.org/sdgs/files/meetings/sdg-inter-workshop-jan-2019/Session%208.a_UNWomen_Gender%20data%20and%20multi%20level%20disaggregation.pdf.
	UNSD. Uganda: User Engagement to Inform the Production of Gender-Related SDG Data (National Priority Gender and Equality Indicators). https://unstats.un.org/sdgs/files/meetings/sdg-inter-workshop-jan-2019/Session%208.b.1_Uganda-User%20Engagement-Case%20for%20NPGEIs-Bangkok%20Jan%202019.pdf.
	UNSD. Bangladesh: Integrated Approach to Producing and Using Gender Statistics for SDG monitoring. https://unstats.un.org/sdgs/files/meetings/sdg-inter-workshop-jan-2019/Session%208.b.2_Bangladesh_Country%20Presentation%20Thailand.pdf.
	UNSD. Viet Nam: SDG from Perspective on Gender Equality. https://unstats.un.org/sdgs/files/meetings/sdg-inter-workshop-jan-2019/Session%208.b.3_Vietnam_SDG%20from%20gender%20equality%20perspective%20in%20Vietnam.pdf.

Topic/Area	Online Resource
Inequality and LNOB analysis: Health equity assessment	UNSD. World Health Organization (WHO): Work on Data Disaggregation (with Introduction to HEAT, HEAT Plus, Other Resources and Illustrations). https://unstats.un.org/sdgs/files/meetings/sdg-inter-workshop-jan-2019/Session%2010.a_WHO%20data%20disaggregtion%20work-Jan%202019%20-%20IAEG_SDG_Bangkok.pdf.
	UNSD. Case study—Uganda. https://unstats.un.org/sdgs/files/meetings/sdg-inter-workshop-jan-2019/Session%2010.b.1_Inequality_In_uganda.pdf.
	UNSD. Case study—Indonesia. https://unstats.un.org/sdgs/files/meetings/sdg-inter-workshop-jan-2019/Session%2010.b.2_indonesia%20experience-AH_nk_rev.pdf.
Inequality and LNOB analysis: Education equity assessment	UNSD. United Nations Educational, Scientific and Cultural Organization (UNESCO) Institute of Statistics: Assessment of Equity in Education. https://unstats.un.org/sdgs/files/meetings/sdg-inter-workshop-jan-2019/Session%2011.a_UNESCO_ESCAP%20data%20disagreegation.pdf.
	UNSD. Rwanda: Education Equity Measurement. https://unstats.un.org/sdgs/files/meetings/sdg-inter-workshop-jan-2019/Session%2011.b.1_Rwanda_SDG%20data%20disaggregation_Education.pdf.
	UNSD. Nepal: Education Equity Assessment- Practices and Experience. https://unstats.un.org/sdgs/files/meetings/sdg-inter-workshop-jan-2019/Session%2011.b.2_Nepal_Education_Equity.pdf.
	UNSD. Philippines: Education Equality in the Philippines. https://unstats.un.org/sdgs/files/meetings/sdg-inter-workshop-jan-2019/Session%2011.b.3_Philippines___Education%20Equality%20AssessmentFINAL4.pdf.
Enabling environment and capacity development	UNSD. Uganda: User Engagement to Inform the Production of Gender-Related SDG Data. https://unstats.un.org/sdgs/files/meetings/sdg-inter-workshop-jan-2019/Session%208.b.1_Uganda-User%20Engagement-Case%20for%20NPGEIs-Bangkok%20Jan%202019.pdf.
	UNSD. Bangladesh: Integrated Approach to Producing and Using Gender Statistics for SDG Monitoring. https://unstats.un.org/sdgs/files/meetings/sdg-inter-workshop-jan-2019/Session%208.b.2_Bangladesh_Country%20Presentation%20Thailand.pdf.

Note: Online resources are subject to change.

**ESCWA Regional Workshop on Data Disaggregation for SDGs Indicators,
19–21 November 2019, Istanbul**
https://www.unescwa.org/events/regional-workshop-data-disaggregation-sdgs-indicators

Topic/Area	Online Resource
Overview of data disaggregation for the SDGs, assessments, general approaches	United Nations Economic and Social Commission for West Asia (ESCWA). Data Disaggregation and the Global Indicator Framework. https://www.unescwa.org/sites/www.unescwa.org/files/u593/1.1_unsd.pdf.
	ESCWA. Data Disaggregation for the SDGs.
	ESCWA. Food and Agriculture Organization of the United Nations (FAO): Disaggregation of the SDG Indicators Related to Food and Agriculture. https://www.unescwa.org/sites/www.unescwa.org/files/u593/2.1_fao.pdf.
	ESCWA. Sudan: SDG Data Gap Analysis. https://www.unescwa.org/sites/www.unescwa.org/files/u593/1.2_sudan.pdf.
Integrating policy demands on inclusive development with data	ESCWA. Module on How Disaggregated Data Shape Policy Formulation. https://www.unescwa.org/sites/www.unescwa.org/files/u593/3.1_escwa.pdf.
	ESCWA. Introduction to EPIC (Every Policy Is Connected). https://www.unescwa.org/sites/www.unescwa.org/files/u593/3.1_epic.pdf.
Sources: Censuses and household surveys	ESCWA. Oman: Using the Census for Disaggregating SDG Indicators. https://www.unescwa.org/sites/www.unescwa.org/files/u593/1.2_oman.pdf.
	ESCWA. Sudan: Surveys and Censuses for Vulnerable Groups Analysis. https://www.unescwa.org/sites/www.unescwa.org/files/u593/2.2_sudan.pdf.
	ESCWA. Morocco: Women and Girls in the Census. https://www.unescwa.org/sites/www.unescwa.org/files/u593/2.2_morocco.pdf.
Sources: SAE	ESCWA. Egypt Poverty Maps. https://www.unescwa.org/sites/www.unescwa.org/files/u593/2.1_egypt.pdf.
Inequality and LNOB analysis	ESCWA. SDG Monitoring on Inequality (SDG 10). https://www.unescwa.org/sites/www.unescwa.org/files/u593/2.1_unsd.pdf.
	ESCWA: Measures of Inequality. https://www.unescwa.org/sites/www.unescwa.org/files/u593/2.1_escwa.pdf.
	ESCWA. Disaggregation of the SDG Indicators Related to Food and Agriculture. https://www.unescwa.org/sites/www.unescwa.org/files/u593/2.1_fao.pdf.
	ESCWA: Examples of Data Analysis and Disaggregation. https://www.unescwa.org/sites/www.unescwa.org/files/u593/2.2_escwa.pdf.
Inequality and LNOB analysis: Health equity assessment	ESCWA. Data Disaggregation for Monitoring Health Inequalities. https://www.unescwa.org/sites/www.unescwa.org/files/u593/2.1_who.pdf.
Inequality and LNOB analysis	ESCWA. SDG Monitoring on Inequality (focus on SDG 10). https://www.unescwa.org/sites/www.unescwa.org/files/u593/2.1_unsd.pdf.
Reporting and communication	ESCWA. How to Create Key Messages and Use Infographics. https://www.unescwa.org/sites/www.unescwa.org/files/u593/3.2_unsd.pdf.
	ESCWA. Qatar Planning and Statistics Authority . Sustainable Development Goals (SDGs) In the State of Qatar. https://www.unescwa.org/sites/www.unescwa.org/files/u593/1.2_sdg_2018_-_qatar_data.xlsx.
SDG data portals	ESCWA. Qatar Planning and Statistics Authority. SDGs State of Qatar. https://sdg-en-psaqatar.opendata.arcgis.com/.

Note: Online resources are subject to change.

REFERENCES

L.P.D. Abitona. 2011. *Provincial Level Estimation of the Proportion of Vitamin A Deficient Children Aged 6 Months to 5 Years in the Philippines.* Unpublished Master's Thesis, University of the Philippines, Los Baños.

Asian Development Bank (ADB). 2017. Data for Development Project. https://www.adb.org/projects/51193-001/main.

ADB. 2019. *Readiness of National Statistical Systems in Asia and the Pacific for Leveraging Big Data to Monitor the SDGs.* ADB Briefs. No. 106. Manila. https://www.adb.org/sites/default/files/publication/491326/adb-brief-106-national-statistical-systems-big-data-sdgs.pdf.

————. 2020. *Introduction to Small Area Estimation Techniques: A Practical Guide for National Statistics Offices.* Manila. https://www.adb.org/sites/default/files/publication/609476/small-area-estimation-guide-nsos.pdf.

————. 2020. *Mapping Poverty through Data Integration and Artificial Intelligence: A Special Supplement of the Key Indicators for Asia and the Pacific 2020.* Manila. https://www.adb.org/sites/default/files/publication/630406/mapping-poverty-ki2020-supplement.pdf.

ADB and United Nations (UN) Economic and Social Commission for Asia and the Pacific (ESCAP). 2017. *Survey on SDG Data Compilation.*

ADB and UN Entity for Gender Equality and the Empowerment of Women (UN Women). 2018. *Gender Equality and the Sustainable Development Goals in Asia and the Pacific: Baseline and Pathways for Transformative Change by 2030.* Bangkok. https://www.adb.org/sites/default/files/publication/461211/gender-equality-sdgs-asia-pacific.pdf.

S.B. Aracid. 2014. *Indirect Estimates of the City and Municipality Level Counts of Underweight Children Aged 0–5 Years in MIMAROPA Region.* Unpublished Undergraduate Special Problem, Institute of Statistics. University of the Philippines, Los Baños.

R.L. Arlan. 2016. *Small Area Estimation of the City and Municipal Level Proportion of 0-5-Year-Old Underweight Children in the Philippines.* Unpublished Master's Thesis, University of the Philippines, Los Baños.

S. Badiee. 2020. *Gender Data Governance and Official Statistics.* Presentation prepared for Counted and Visible: Global conference on the measurement of gender equality and intersecting inequalities. New

York. 26–27 February. https://data.unwomen.org/sites/default/files/documents/gender%20and%20 intersecting%20inequalities/docs/presentations/2.8.1.%20Open%20data%20watch.pdf.

A. Bidarbakht-Nia. 2018. Policy-Data Integration: Key to achieving the SDGs for all. *UN ESCAP Statistics Division Working Paper Series*. SD/WP/07/April 2018. Bangkok. https://www.unescap.org/sites/default/ d8files/knowledge-products/SD_Working_Paper_no.7_Apr2018_Policy-Data_Integration.pdf.

————. 2018. *Why, What and How of Policy – Data Integration*. Presentation prepared for the Pacific Workshop on Developing a Generic Tool for Policy–Data Integration. Fiji. 19–21 March 2018. https://www.unescap.org/sites/default/files/S3%20-%20Policy%20Statistics_Data%20integration.pdf.

————. 2018. Connecting policymakers and data producers. *UN ESCAP blog*. 22 August. https://www.unescap.org/blog/connecting-policymakers-and-data-producers.

A. Bidarbakht-Nia, C. Ryan, and S. Serrao. 2019. *Every Policy Is Connected (EPIC): A generic tool for policy-data integration*. UN ESCAP Statistics Division Working Paper Series. SD/WP/09/September 2019. Bangkok. https://www.unescap.org/sites/default/d8files/knowledge-products/SD_Working_Paper_ no.9_Sep2019_EPIC_tool.pdf.

D. Buono et al. 2018. *Enhanced step-by-step approach for the use of big data in modelling for official statistics*. Paper prepared for the 16th conference of the International Association for Official Statistics. 19–21 September. Paris.

Centers for Disease Prevention and Control. https://www.cdc.gov/reproductivehealth/global/tools/ surveys.htm.

Community-Based Monitoring System Act (Republic Act No. 11315). https://www.officialgazette.gov.ph/ downloads/2019/04apr/20190417-RA-11315-RRD.pdf.

G. De Silva et al. 2019. *Improving data availability for economic empowerment of women in Sri Lanka: A study on data integration for monitoring the SDGs*. Paper prepared for Asia-Pacific Economic Statistics Week 2019. 17–19 June. Bangkok. https://communities.unescap.org/system/files/improving_data_ availability_for_economic_empowerment_of_women_in_sri_lanka.pdf.

The DHS Program. https://www.dhsprogram.com/.

————. https://www.statcompiler.com/en/.

Economic Commission for Latin America and the Caribbean. 2019. Second meeting of the Statistical Coordination Group for the 2030 Agenda in Latin America and the Caribbean: *Disaggregated data for regional monitoring of the SDGs*. 3–5 September 2019. Quito, Ecuador. https://www.cepal.org/en/events/ second-meeting-statistical-coordination-group-2030-agenda-latin-americaand-caribbean.

Expert Group on Refugee and Internally Displaced Persons Statistics (EGRIS). 2018. *International Recommendations on Refugee Statistics*. https://unstats.un.org/unsd/demographic-social/Standards-and-Methods/files/Principles_and_Recommendations/International-Migration/2018_1746_EN_08-E.pdf.

————. 2020. *Compilers' Manual on Displacement Statistics*. Background document prepared for the 51st session of the Statistical Commission. 3–6 March. New York. https://unstats.un.org/unsd/statcom/51st-session/documents/BG-item-3n-compilers-manual-E.pdf.

L. Farkas. 2017. *Analysis and comparative review of equality data collection practices in the European Union: Data Collection in the Field of Ethnicity*. Luxembourg, p. 21. https://ec.europa.eu/newsroom/just/document.cfm?action=display&doc_id=45791.

Flowminder Foundation. 2018. *Spatial Models for Slum Area Mapping*. Presentation prepared for the United Nations Global Geospatial Information Management meeting. 30 November. Nairobi. http://ggim.un.org/meetings/2018-International-Seminar-Kenya/documents/03_thomson_v3.pdf.

Food and Agriculture Organization of the United Nations. 2015. *World Programme for the Census of Agriculture 2020. Volume 1. Programme, concepts, and definitions*. https://ec.europa.eu/eurostat/ramon/statmanuals/files/world_census_agri_2020_EN.pdf.

————. 2016. *Agri-Gender Statistics Toolkit*. Ankara. http://www.fao.org/3/i5769e/i5769e.pdf.

————. 2019. *Integrated Approach Program on Food Security*. https://www.thegef.org/project/food-iap-fostering-sustainability-and-resilience-food-security-sub-saharan-africa-integrated.

————. 2021. *Guidelines on data disaggregation for SDG Indicators using survey data*. Rome. http://www.fao.org/3/cb3253en/CB3253EN.pdf.

Gartner. *Information Technology Glossary*. Big Data. https://www.gartner.com/it-glossary/big-data/.

Geo-referenced Infrastructure and Demographic Data for Development. 2020. *High resolution population estimates*. https://grid3.org/solution/high-resolution-population-estimates.

Global Partnership for Sustainable Development Data. 2018. *Inclusive Data Charter vision and principles*. https://www.data4sdgs.org/sites/default/files/2018-08/IDC_onepager_Final.pdf.

————. Data4SDGs Toolbox. https://www.data4sdgs.org/initiatives/data4sdgs-toolbox (accessed 14 October 2020).

————. 2019. *Choosing and engaging with citizen-generated data*. https://www.data4sdgs.org/sites/default/files/services_files/Choosing%20and%20Engaging%20with%20CGD_The%20Guide_0.pdf.

————. 2019. *Inclusive Data Charter Initiative (Annual Monitoring) 2019: Philippine Statistics Authority. Authority*. https://www.data4sdgs.org/sites/default/files/2019-07/PSA%20-%20IDC%20annual%20monitoring%20form%202019.pdf.

Global Strategy Improving Agricultural & Rural Statistics. http://gsars.org/en/tag/geoinfo/.

Government of Cambodia, National Institute of Statistics. 2019. *Cambodia Experience in Producing Disaggregated Data for SDGs*. Presentation prepared for the International Workshop on Data Disaggregation for the SDGs. Bangkok. 28–30 January. https://unstats.un.org/sdgs/files/meetings/

sdg-inter-workshop-jan-2019/Session%202.b.1_Cambodia_Experience%20in%20producing%20 disaggregated%20data%20for%20SDGs.pdf.

Government of Canada, Statistics Canada. 2020. Transparency and accountability. *Statistics Canada and disaggregated data*. https://www.statcan.gc.ca/eng/transparency-accountability/disaggregated-data.

Government of Ethiopia, Central Statistical Agency. 2019. *Data Disaggregation Practice on National SDG Implementation in Ethiopia*. Presentation prepared for the International Workshop on Data Disaggregation for the SDGs. Bangkok. 28–30 January. https://unstats.un.org/sdgs/files/meetings/sdg-inter-workshop-jan-2019/Session%202.b.2_%20Ethiopia%20Data%20Disaggregation%20Practice%20on%20 National%20SDG.pdf.

Government of Turkmenistan, State Committee of Turkmenistan on Statistics. 2019. *Data Disaggregation for SDGs: Turkmenistan's Experience*. Presentation prepared for the International Workshop on Data Disaggregation for the SDGs. Bangkok. 28–30 January. https://unstats.un.org/sdgs/files/meetings/sdg-inter-workshop-jan-2019/Session%202.b.3_Turkmenistan_Bang_270119%20ENG%20PRINT.pdf.

J. Haughton and S. Khandker. 2009. *Handbook on Poverty and Inequality*. Washington, DC: The World Bank. http://documents1.worldbank.org/curated/en/488081468157174849/pdf/483380PUB0Pove101 OFFICIAL0USE0ONLY1.pdf.

B. Hellali. 2018. *Hybrid census to generate spatially-disaggregated population estimates*. https://unstats. un.org/unsd/undataforum/blog/hybrid-census-to-generate-spatially-disaggregated-population-estimates/.

A.R. Hosseinpoor et al. 2018. Capacity building for health inequality monitoring in Indonesia: enhancing the equity orientation of country health information systems. *Global Health Action*. 11 (supplement 1). pp. 7–12. https://doi.org/10.1080/16549716.2017.1419739.

Idea Maps Network. 2020. *Integrated Deprived Area "Slum" Mapping System*. Presentation prepared for the 6th Conference on Big Data for Official Statistics. 31 August–2 September. Virtual conference. https://unstats.un.org/unsd/bigdata/conferences/2020/presentations/day2/session6/Ms.%20 Dana%20Thompson.pdf.

International Household Survey Network. National Data Archive survey cataloguing software. http://www.ihsn.org/projects/NADA-development.

International Organization for Migration. 2018. *A pilot study on disaggregating SDG indicators by migratory Status*. Geneva. https://publications.iom.int/system/files/pdf/a_pilot_study_on_disaggregating_sdg_ indicators.pdf.

S. Klasen and M. Fleurbaey. 2018. Leaving no one behind: Some conceptual and empirical issues. *UN Department of Economic and Social Affairs Committee for Development Policy Background Papers*. ST/ ESA/2018/CDP/44. New York. https://www.un.org/development/desa/dpad/wp-content/uploads/ sites/45/publication/CDP_BP44_June_2018.pdf.

LSMS. https://www.worldbank.org/en/programs/lsms.

A. Martinez Jr. 2019. *Small Area Estimation and Big Data.* Presentation prepared for the International Workshop on Sustainable Development Goal Data Disaggregation. Bangkok. 28–30 January. https://unstats.un.org/sdgs/files/meetings/sdg-inter-workshop-jan-2019/Session%207.a_ADB_Small%20Area%20Estimation%20-%20jan29.pdf.

Merriam-Webster English Dictionary. https://www.merriam-webster.com/dictionary/big%20data.

Merriam-Webster English Dictionary. https://www.merriam-webster.com/dictionary/intersectionality.

MICS. http://mics.unicef.org.

L. Morales and T. Orrell. 2019. *Data Interoperability: A Practitioner's Guide to Joining up Data in the Development Sector.* http://www.data4sdgs.org/sites/default/files/services_files/Interoperability%20-%20A%20practitioner%E2%80%99s%20guide%20to%20joining-up%20data%20in%20the%20development%20sector.pdf.

S. Muchlisoh et al. 2015. Estimation of unemployment rate using small area estimation model based on a rotating panel national labor force survey. *Indonesian Journal of Statistics.* 20 (2). pp. 1–4. http://journal.ipb.ac.id/index.php/statistika/article/download/16755/12206.

I.D.P. Nuestro. 2014. *Municipal and City Level Estimation of the Total Number of Maternal Deaths in MIMAROPA.* Unpublished Undergraduate Special Problem, Institute of Statistics. University of the Philippines, Los Baños.

Open Data Watch. *Open Data to Support Sustainable Development Goals.* https://opendatawatch.com/publications/open-data-to-support-sustainable-development-goals/.

Oxford English Dictionary. https://www.lexico.com/definition/proof_of_concept.

Partnership in Statistics for Development in the 21st Century (PARIS21) and UN High-level Group for Partnership, Coordination and Capacity-Building for Statistics for the 2030 Agenda for Sustainable Development. 2018. *Survey Results: New Approaches to Capacity Development and Future Priorities.* Paris. https://paris21.org/capacity-development-40/cd40-survey.

PARIS21 and UN Women. 2020. *Assessing Data and Statistical Capacity Gaps for Better Gender Statistics: Framework and Implementation Guidelines.* https://paris21.org/sites/default/files/inline-files/Framework%202020_update_web_0.pdf.

————. Forthcoming. *Guidelines for Integrating Gender in National Strategies for Development of Statistics.* https://nsdsguidelines.paris21.org/node/608.

PARIS21. ADAPT Gender Module. https://paris21.org/sites/default/files/inline-files/Gender_ADAPT_2pp_A5.pdf.

————. ADAPT. https://paris21.org/advanced-data-planning-tool-adapt.

————. Citizen-Generated Data. https://paris21.org/cgd.

————. NSDS Guidelines. https://nsdsguidelines.paris21.org/.

————. Supporting Gender Statistics. https://paris21.org/supporting-gender-statistics.

————. 2020. *Citizen-generated gender data in Maldives: connecting data ecosystems.* News release. 10 June. https://paris21.org/news-center/news/citizen-generated-gender-data-maldives-connecting-data-ecosystems.

————. 2020. *Guidelines for Developing Statistical Capacity: A Roadmap for Capacity Development 4.0.* https://paris21.org/sites/default/files/inline-files/UNV003_Guidelines%20for%20Capacity%20Development%20PRINT_0.pdf.

————. 2020. *Making Gender Statistics a Top Priority in the Senegalese National Strategy for Development of Statistics.* News release. 11 March. https://paris21.org/news-center/news/making-gender-statistics-top-priority-senegalese-national-strategy-development.

————. 2020. *New report shares insights on using citizen-generated data for SDG reporting in the Philippines.* News release. 4 August. https://paris21.org/news-center/news/new-report-shares-insights-using-citizen-generated-data-sdg-reporting-philippines.

Philippine Statistics Authority (PSA). 2009. *2003 City and Municipal Level Poverty Estimates.* https://psa.gov.ph/sites/default/files/2003%20SAE%20of%20poverty%20%28Full%20Report%29_0.pdf.

————. 2016. *2012 Municipal and City Level Poverty Estimates.* Manila.

————. 2019. *2018 Family Income and Expenditure Survey.* https://psa.gov.ph/content/annual-family-income-estimated-php-313-thousand-average-2018.

————. 2020. *Farmers, Fisherfolks, Individuals Residing in Rural Areas and Children Posted the Highest Poverty Incidences Among the Basic Sectors in 2018.* News release. 3 June. https://psa.gov.ph/sites/default/files/Press%20Release%20-%20Poverty%20Incidences%20Among%20the%20Basic%20Sectors%20in%202018_signed_1.pdf.

————. 2020. *Relating Rural Access Index and Poverty in the Philippines.* Presentation prepared for the 6th Conference on Big Data for Official Statistics. 31 August–2 September. Virtual conference. https://unstats.un.org/unsd/bigdata/conferences/2020/presentations/day2/session6/Mr.%20Justin%20Angelo.pdf.

C.E.N. Relente. 2010. *Municipal and City Level Estimation of the Number of Underweight 0-5-Year-Old Children in Bicol Region.* Unpublished Undergraduate Special Problem, Institute of Statistics.University of the Philippines, Los Baños.

P. Seck. 2020. *Integrate intersecting inequalities to leave no one behind.* United Nations World Data Forum Blog. 13 October. https://unstats.un.org/unsd/undataforum/blog/Integrate-intersecting-inequalities-to-leave-no-one-behind/.

C. Smith, A. Mashadi, and L. Capra. 2013. *Ubiquitous sensing for mapping poverty in developing countries.* http://www0.cs.ucl.ac.uk/staff/l.capra/publications/d4d.pdf.

StaTact. About StaTact. https://statact.unitar.org/en/about-statact.

Statistics Indonesia. 2020. *Using Big Data for SDGs: Mobile Data for Tourism and Commuting.* Presentation prepared for the prepared for the 6th International Conference on Big Data for Official Statistics. 31 August–2 September. Virtual conference. https://unstats.un.org/unsd/bigdata/conferences/2020/presentations/day1/session3/Use%20of%20Mobile%20Phone%20for%20SDGs_rev2.0.pdf.

Statistics Korea and SK Telecom. 2020. *Mobile Data for Tourism, Migration, Population and Transport in Korea.* Presentation prepared for the 6th International Conference on Big Data for Official Statistics. 31 August–2 September. Virtual conference. https://unstats.un.org/unsd/bigdata/conferences/2020/presentations/day1/session3/1.%20Dongok%20Lee.pdf.

Statistics New Zealand. 2015. *Data and Statistics integration manual: 2nd edition.* Wellington. https://ndhadeliver.natlib.govt.nz/delivery/DeliveryManagerServlet?dps_pid=IE25102655; New Zealand. Integrated data. https://www.stats.govt.nz/integrated-data/.

Statistics Sweden. 2020. *Annual statistical review with a focus on LNOB.* Presentation prepared for the 11th IAEG-SDGs Meeting. 4 November 2020. https://unstats.un.org/sdgs/files/meetings/iaeg-sdgs-meeting-11/13b.%20Sweden-first%20country%20report%20with%20a%20focus%20on%20vulnerable%20populations_Sweden.pdf.

————. 2020. *Statistical review focusing on the principle of leaving no one behind.* Paper prepared for the United Nations Economic Commission for Europe (UNECE) Expert Meeting on Statistics for SDGs. 22–27 April 2020. https://unece.org/fileadmin/DAM/stats/documents/ece/ces/ge.32/2020/mtg1/W_1_2_ENG_Sweden-Statistical_review_focusing_on_the_principle_of_Leaving_no_one_behind.pdf.

SDGs Global Dashboard. https://www.sdgsdashboard.org.

United Nations (UN). *Glossary of Classification Terms.* https://unstats.un.org/unsd/classifications/bestpractices/glossary_short.pdf.

UN. 2015. *Transforming our world: the 2030 Agenda for Sustainable Development* (para. 1). https://sustainabledevelopment.un.org/post2015/transformingourworld.

————. 2015. *The Millennium Development Goals Report 2015.* New York. http://www.un.org/millenniumgoals/2015_MDG_Report/pdf/MDG%202015%20rev%20(July%201).pdf.

————. 2017. *Global indicator framework for the Sustainable Development Goals and targets of the 2030 Agenda for Sustainable Development.* https://unstats.un.org/sdgs/indicators/Global%20Indicator%20Framework%20after%202020%20review_Eng.pdf.

———. 2020. *Background document for the Note by the Secretary-General transmitting the report of the Global Working Group on Big Data for Official Statistics* (E/CN.3/2020/24). Document prepared for the 51st session of the Statistical Commission. 3–6 March. New York. https://unstats.un.org/unsd/statcom/51st-session/documents/UN_BigData_report_v6.0-E.html.

UN Committee of Experts on Global Geospatial Information Management for Europe. 2019. *The territorial dimension in SDG indicators: geospatial data analysis and its integration with statistical data.* Lisbon. https://un-ggim-europe.org/wp-content/uploads/2019/05/UN_GGIM_08_05_2019-The-territorial-dimension-in-SDG-indicators-Final.pdf.

UN Department of Economic and Social Affairs (DESA). *Enhancing national statistical capacity to measure, monitor, assess and report on progress on achieving post-2015 goals and targets for sustainable development.* https://www.un.org/development/desa/capacity-development/projects/project/statistical-capacity-for-progress-on-sdgs/.

United Nations Development Programme (UNDP). 2017. *SDG Dashboards: The role of information tools in the implementation of the 2030 Agenda.* Draft for comments. http://www.asia-pacific.undp.org/content/dam/rbap/docs/meetTheSDGs/SDG%20Dashboards%20UNDP-SIGOB.pdf.

UNDP. 2018. *What does it mean to leave no one behind? A UNDP discussion paper and framework for implementation.* New York. https://www.undp.org/content/undp/en/home/librarypage/poverty-reduction/what-does-it-mean-to-leave-no-one-behind-.html.

UN Economic Commission for Europe (UNECE). 2013. *What Does "Big Data" Mean for Official Statistics?* https://statswiki.unece.org/download/attachments/58492100/Big+Data+HLG+Final.docx?version=1&modificationDate=1362939424184.

———. 2018. *A Guide to Data Integration for Official Statistics.* https://statswiki.unece.org/spaces/flyingpdf/pdfpageexport.action?pageId=129171769.

———. 2019. *Disability Statistics: Joint report of the Secretary-General, the Washington Group on Disability Statistics and international agencies.* Geneva. https://unstats.un.org/unsd/statcom/51st-session/documents/2020-34-DisabilityStats-Rev-EE.pdf.

———. 2019. *Guidance on Data Integration for Measuring Migration.* Geneva. http://www.unece.org/fileadmin/DAM/stats/publications/2018/ECECESSTAT20186.pdf.

UNECE and the Conference of European Statisticians. 2017. *In-depth review of data integration.* Note prepared for the meeting of the Conference of European Statisticians 2016/2017 Bureau. 14–15 February. Geneva. http://www.unece.org/fileadmin/DAM/stats/documents/ece/ces/bur/2017/February/02_in-depth_review_data_integration_final.pdf.

UN Economic Commission for Latin America and the Caribbean. https://www.cepal.org/en/events/second-meeting-statistical-coordination-group-2030-agenda-latin-america-and-caribbean.

UN ESCAP. 2019. *Integrated Statistics: A journey worthwhile.* Stats Brief. Issue no. 19. https://www.unescap.org/sites/default/files/Stats_Brief_Issue19_Jul2019_Integrated_Statistics.pdf.

UN Economic and Social Commission for Western Asia. 2019. https://www.unescwa.org/events/regional-workshop-data-disaggregation-sdgs-indicators.

UN General Assembly. 2014. *Resolution adopted by the General Assembly on 29 January 2014: Fundamental Principles of Official Statistics Resolution (68/261)*. New York. https://unstats.un.org/unsd/dnss/gp/FP-New-E.pdf.

————. 2015. *Resolution adopted by the General Assembly on 25 September 2015: Transforming our world—the 2030 Agenda for Sustainable Development (70/1)*. New York. p. 6. https://www.un.org/en/development/desa/population/migration/generalassembly/docs/globalcompact/A_RES_70_1_E.pdf.

————. 2017. *Resolution adopted by the General Assembly on 10 July 2017: Work of the Statistical Commission pertaining to the 2030 Agenda for Sustainable Development Resolution (71/313)*. New York. https://undocs.org/A/RES/71/313.

UN Global Geospatial Information Management Secretariat. 2019. *The Global Statistical Geospatial Framework*. New York. http://ggim.un.org/meetings/GGIM-committee/9th-Session/documents/The_GSGF.pdf.

UN Global Pulse. 2012. *Big Data for Development: Challenges and Opportunities*. New York. https://www.unglobalpulse.org/wp-content/uploads/2012/05/BigDataforDevelopment-UNGlobalPulseMay2012.pdf.

UN Global SDG Database. https://unstats.un.org/sdgs/indicators/database/.

UN Global Working Group on Big Data for Official Statistics' Task Team on Training, Competencies and Capacity Development. 2020. *Global assessment of institutional readiness for the use of big data in official statistics*. https://unstats.un.org/bigdata/task-teams/training/UN_BigData_report_v5.0.html.

————. Task Team on Training, Competencies and Capacity Development. https://unstats.un.org/bigdata/task-teams/training/index.cshtml.

————. 2020. *Competency Framework for Big Data Acquisition and Processing*. https://unstats.un.org/bigdata/task-teams/training/UNGWG_Competency_Framework.pdf.

UN High-level Group for Partnership, Coordination and Capacity-Building for Statistics for the 2030 Agenda for Sustainable Development. 2017. *Cape Town Global Action Plan for Sustainable Development Data*. https://unstats.un.org/sdgs/hlg/Cape-Town-Global-Action-Plan/.

UN High Level Political Forum (HLPF). https://sustainabledevelopment.un.org/hlpf.

————. VNRs. https://sustainabledevelopment.un.org/vnrs/.

————. 2018. *Summary of Learning Session at 2018 High-Level Political Forum*. New York. 11 July. https://sustainabledevelopment.un.org/hlpf/2018.

————. 2018. *Supporting an integrated implementation of the SDGs: Tools for addressing SDG connections and enhancing policy and institutional coherence.* Presentation prepared for the 2018 High-Level Political Forum. New York. 11 July.

UNHCR. 2018. Refugee Data Finder. Methodology. https://www.unhcr.org/refugee-statistics/methodology.

UNICEF. MICS Compiler. https://mics.unicef.org/tools.

UN Human Settlements Programme. 2019. *The Urban SDG Monitoring Series.* Issue 1. February 2019. http://unhabitat.org.ir/wp-content/uploads/2019/03/SDG-11.1.1-Newsletter_2.1.pdf.

UN OHCHR. 2015. *Transforming Our World: Human Rights in the 2030 Agenda for Sustainable Development.* https://www.ohchr.org/Documents/Issues/MDGs/Post2015/TransformingOurWorld.pdf.

————. 2018. *A Human Rights-Based Approach to Data: Leaving No One Behind in the 2030 Agenda for Sustainable Development—Guidance Note to Data Collection and Disaggregation.* Geneva. https://www.ohchr.org/Documents/Issues/HRIndicators/GuidanceNoteonApproachtoData.pdf.

————. 2018. *International human rights standards and recommendations relevant to the disaggregation of SDG indicators.* https://unstats.un.org/sdgs/files/meetings/iaeg-sdgs-meeting-07/Human%20Rights%20Standards%20for%20Data%20Disaggregation%20-%20OHCHR%20-%20Background%20Document.pdf.

UN Population Fund. 2017. *New Methodology: a hybrid census to generate spatially disaggregated population estimates—Technical Brief.* https://www.unfpa.org/sites/default/files/resource-pdf/Hybrid_Census_Brief_v9.pdf.

UNSC. https://unstats.un.org/unsd/statcom/.

UN Statistics Division (UNSD). SDG Indicators Metadata Repository. https://unstats.un.org/sdgs/metadata/?Text=&Goal=17&Target=17.18.

UNSD. UNSD- Foreign, Commonwealth & Development Office Project on SDG Monitoring. https://unstats.un.org/capacity-development/UNSD-FCDO/.

UNSD and Inter-agency and Expert Group on Sustainable Development Goal Indicators (IAEG-SDGs). 2020. *Draft Compilation of tools/guidance of existing materials for data disaggregation.* https://unstats.un.org/sdgs/files/meetings/iaeg-sdgs-meeting-11/Compilation%20of%20tools.guidance%20of%20existing%20materials%20for%20data%20disaggregation-%20DRAFT.pdf. (accessed 9 March 2021).

————. IAEG-SDGs. https://unstats.un.org/sdgs/iaeg-sdgs.

UNSD. IAEG-SDGs Working Group on SDMX. https://unstats.un.org/sdgs/iaeg-sdgs/sdmx-working-group/.

————. IAEG-SDGs. 2019. *Data Disaggregation for the SDG Indicators.* https://unstats.un.org/sdgs/iaeg-sdgs/disaggregation/.

————. IAEG-SDGs. *Improving data flows and global data reporting for the Sustainable Development Goals.* https://unstats.un.org/sdgs/iaeg-sdgs/data-flows/.

————. 2019. IAEG-SDGs. *Annex I of Data Disaggregation for the SDG Indicators: Compilation on Data Disaggregation Dimensions and Categories for Global SDG Indicators.* https://unstats.un.org/sdgs/files/Annex%201%20-%20Disaggregation%20Compilation.xlsx.

————. IAEG-SDGs. *Annex II of Data Disaggregation for the SDG Indicators: Summary of Disaggregation Dimensions and Categories Available and Planned in Global SDG Indicator Database.* https://unstats.un.org/sdgs/files/Annex%202%20-%20Disaggregation%20Availability.xlsx.

————. 2001. *Principles and Recommendations for a Vital Statistics System, Revision 2.* New York. p. 37. https://unstats.un.org/unsd/demographic-social/Standards-and-Methods/files/Principles_and_Recommendations/CRVS/SeriesM_19rev2-E.pdf.

————. 2012. *Knowledgebase on Economic Statistics: Methods and Country Practices.* UNECE "Making Data Meaningful" guide series: Parts 1, 2, and 3. https://unstats.un.org/unsd/EconStatKB/KnowledgebaseArticle10350.aspx.

————. 2016. *The Sustainable Development Goals Report.* https://unstats.un.org/sdgs/report/2016/leaving-no-one-behind.

————. 2016. *Report of the 2015 Big Data Survey.* Background document prepared for the 47th session of the Statistical Commission. 8–11 March. New York. https://unstats.un.org/bigdata/documents/reports/GWG%20Background%20document%20-%202016%20-6-Report-of-the-2015-Big-Data-Survey-E.pdf.

————. 2017. *The Sustainable Development Goals Report.* https://unstats.un.org/sdgs/report/2017/overview/.

————. 2018. *Overview of standards for data disaggregation.* https://unstats.un.org/sdgs/files/Overview%20of%20Standards%20for%20Data%20Disaggregation.pdf.

————. 2018. *Summary of IAEG-SDGs Working Meeting on Data Disaggregation.* Paper prepared for the Eighth Meeting of the Inter-Agency and Expert Group on the Sustainable Development Goal Indicators. 9 November. Stockholm. https://unstats.un.org/sdgs/files/Data%20disaggregation%20working%20meeting%20Summary_final.pdf.

————. 2018. *Use of administrative data for official statistics: The Global Perspective.* Beijing. 26-29 June 2018. Presentation prepared for the International Workshop on Sustainable Development Indicators. https://unstats.un.org/sdgs/files/meetings/sdg-inter-workshop-june-2018/Day2_Session3_Adm%20Data_UNSD.pdf.

————. 2019. *New data sources for official statistics – access, use and new skills.* Note prepared for the Economic Commission for Europe's Conference of European Statisticians, 67th plenary session. Paris. 26–28 June. https://unece.org/fileadmin/DAM/stats/documents/ece/ces/2019/ECE_CES_2019_41.pdf.

————. 2019. International Workshop on Data Disaggregation for SDGs. 28–30 January 2019. Bangkok, Thailand. https://unstats.un.org/sdgs/meetings/sdg-inter-workshop-jan-2019/.

————. 2020. *Technical Report: Measuring Sustainable Development Goals Indicators through Population and Housing Censuses and Civil Registration and Vital Statistics Data.* Draft as of 12 October 2020. https://www.unescwa.org/sites/www.unescwa.org/files/u1461/measuring_sdgs_through_phc_and_crvs_data.pdf.

————. 2020. *E-Handbook on Sustainable Development Goals Indicators.* https://unstats.un.org/wiki/display/SDGeHandbook/Home.

UN Women. 2018. *Turning Promises into Action: Gender Equality in the 2030 Agenda for Sustainable Development.* New York. https://www.unwomen.org/-/media/headquarters/attachments/sections/library/publications/2018/sdg-report-gender-equality-in-the-2030-agenda-for-sustainable-development-2018-en.pdf?la=en&vs=4332.

————. 2019. *Gender data and multi-level disaggregation: an LNOB perspective to SDG monitoring.* Presentation prepared for the International Workshop on Data Disaggregation for Sustainable Development Goals. 29 January. Bangkok. https://unstats.un.org/sdgs/files/meetings/sdg-inter-workshop-jan-2019/Session%208.a_UNWomen_Gender%20data%20and%20multi%20level%20disaggregation.pdf.

————. 2020. *Module 7: Multilevel Disaggregation Analysis to Monitor the SDGs from a Leave No One Behind Perspective—Training Syllabus.* https://data.unwomen.org/sites/default/files/documents/Asia-Pacific-Training-Curriculum/Module7/Module7_Syllabus_LNOB.pdf.

————. 2020. *Counted and Visible: Global Conference on the measurement of gender and intersecting inequalities.* https://data.unwomen.org/news/counted-and-visible-global-conference-measurement-gender-and-intersecting-inequalities.

UN Women and Intersecretariat Working Group on Household Surveys. 2021. *Counted and Visible: Toolkit to Better Utilize Existing Household Surveys to Generate Disaggregated Gender Statistics.* https://data.unwomen.org/resources/counted-and-visible-toolkit.

Uganda Bureau of Statistics, and UNICEF. 2018. *Poverty Maps of Uganda: Mapping the Spatial Distribution of Poor Households Based on Data from the 2012/13 Uganda National Household Survey and the 2014 National Housing and Population Census—Technical Report.* http://documents1.worldbank.org/curated/en/456801530034180435/pdf/Poverty-Maps-Report.pdf.

United States Census Bureau. 2018. *Sustainable Development Goals and the 2020 Round of Censuses. Select Topics in International Censuses.* https://www.census.gov/content/dam/Census/library/working-papers/2018/demo/sdg-2020.pdf.

———. 2019. Counting the Hard to Count in a Census. *Select Topics in International Censuses.* https://www.census.gov/content/dam/Census/library/working-papers/2019/demo/Hard-to-Count-Populations-Brief.pdf.

———. 2020. Classification and Delineation of Urban Areas in a Census. *Select Topics in International Censuses.* https://www.census.gov/content/dam/Census/library/working-papers/2020/demo/urban-stic.pdf.

Y. Wang. 2019. *Report: DHS and Geo-covariates data integration—Case study on Bangladesh survey 2014.* https://communities.unescap.org/system/files/report_dhs_and_geo-covariates_data_integration_bangladesh_survey_2014.pdf.

N. A. Wardrop, W. C. Jochem, T. J. Bird, H. R. Chamberlain, D. Clarke, D. Kerr, L. Bengtsson, S. Juran, V. Seaman, and A. J. Tatem. 2018. *Spatially disaggregated population estimates in the absence of national population and housing census data.* Proceedings of the National Academy of Sciences Apr 2018, 115 (14) 3529-3537. https://www.pnas.org/content/115/14/3529.

R. Van der Weide. 2017. *Poverty Mapping at the World Bank.* Manila. https://psa.gov.ph/content/session-2-1-mr-roy-van-der-weide.

Washington Group on Disability Statistics. 2018. *Background Document prepared by the Washington Group on Disability Statistics for the 49th Session of the United Nations Statistical Commission.* https://unstats.un.org/unsd/statcom/49th-session/documents/BG-Item3n-WG-on-Disability-Statistics-E.pdf.

———. *Disaggregation and SDGs.* https://www.washingtongroup-disability.com/resources/disaggregation-and-sdgs/.

World Bank. ADePT. https://www.worldbank.org/en/topic/health/brief/adept-resource-center.

World Bank WDI. 2021. https://data.worldbank.org/indicator/SH.H2O.SMDW.RU.ZS (accessed 21 January 2021).

World Data Lab. 2019. Presentation prepared for the International Workshop on Data Disaggregation for SDGs. 28-30 January. Bangkok, Thailand. https://unstats.un.org/sdgs/files/meetings/sdg-inter-workshop-jan-2019/Session%207.b_World%20Data%20Lab.pdf.

World Health Organization. (WHO). HEAT. https://www.who.int/gho/health_equity/assessment_toolkit/en/.

———. HEAT: Built-in database edition, version 3.1. https://whoequity.shinyapps.io/HEAT/. (accessed 9 March 2021).

———. Health Equity Assessment Toolkit. https://www.who.int/data/gho/health-equity/assessment_toolkit.

———. Health Equity Monitor Database. https://www.who.int/data/gho/health-equity/health-equity-monitor-database.

————. MDS. https://www.who.int/disabilities/data/mds/en/.

————. 2013. *Handbook on Health Inequality Monitoring: with a Special Focus on Low- and Middle-Income Countries*. Geneva. https://apps.who.int/iris/bitstream/handle/10665/85345/9789241548632_eng.pdf.

————. 2015. *eLearning module on health inequality monitoring*. https://extranet.who.int/elearn/course/category.php?id=15.

————. 2017. *State of Health Inequality: Indonesia*. Geneva. https://apps.who.int/iris/bitstream/handle/10665/259685/9789241513340-eng.pdf.

————. Global Health Observatory Data. https://www.who.int/data/gho.

A. Yazdani. 2019. *Using Data Integration to Meet the Ambitions of the 2030 Agenda*. United Nations Economic and Social Commission for Asia and the Pacific blog. 3 July. https://www.unescap.org/blog/using-data-integration-meet-ambitions-2030-agenda.

X. Zhang, S. Onufrak, J. Holt, and J. Croft. 2013. *A Multilevel Approach to Estimating Small Area Childhood Obesity Prevalence at the Census Block-Group Level. Prev Chronic Dis 2013*;10:120252. https://www.cdc.gov/pcd/issues/2013/12_0252.htm.